Contents

List of Photographs	iv
Introduction	v
Acknowledgements	v
Part 1 Familienforschung Jorss	**1**
Part 2 The Biography of John Frederick Benton	**43**
Part 3 Conclusion	**160**

Appendix 1 — 4

1. Jorss "family tree" — 5
2. CV of Chris Jorss — 6
3. Copy of death certificate of Chris Jorss — 7
4. Note from the archival files in Lubeck — 8
5. Report on the voyage of the "Fritz Reuter", Hamburg to New Zealand, 1874 — 9–10
6. The ticket and health certificates issued to Chris Jorss for his journey — 11–12
7. A list of photographs taken by Chris Jorss whilst in New Zealand en route to Sydney, Australia — 14
8. A series of letters written by Chris Jorss and his wife to their children Anne and John in 1903/1904 — 15–25
9. A note of rent paid in 1885 and the trace on the chemist's address in London — 26
10. The extract from the book:– "The Mechanical Eye in Australia—", and a copy of the advertisement in the Cootamundra Herald, 1880 — 27–28
11. The facsimile of the first two pages of Chris Jorss's personal photographic notebook dated 1875 – 1885, with translation. — 29–32

Appendix 2 — 55

1. The identity papers of John Frederick Benton, including his death certificate
2. The two wills of John Benton — 63–64
3. Papers relating to J Benton's schooling in Australia — 65–66
4. Papers relating to J Benton's schooling in England — 67–72
5. Papers relating to J Benton's career with Marconi and his trip to Angola — 73–102
6. Some recent letters written by people who knew John Benton — 103–107
7. A collection of documents relating to the flying field at Chalvey, Slough 108
8. The Press report on the "Air Car" — 116
9. Descriptions of the aeroplanes built by Benton and Allen — 117–120
10. A list of Patents taken out by Benton — 121–139
11. A series of letters dated 1915 – 1916, relating to the efforts made by John Benton to sell his ideas and aeroplanes to various military bodies. The letters also include some personal ones to his friends who helped him in his work — 140
12. Newspaper announcement of Admiralty Inventions Board — 159

Appendix 3 — 162

1. The Patent taken out by J Benton referring to "Articles of adornment and method of producing same". — 162

Photographs

1	The Marconi School of Wireless, Frinton-on-Sea.	35
2	The Marconi works at Chelmsford.	35
3a	The 'Air Car' at Chalvey, 1911.	36
3b	The 'Air Car' at Chalvey, 1911.	37
4	J. F. Benton seated in the B.6 at Chalvey.	38
5a	The factory at 58, King Street, Maidenhead, November 11th, 1918.	39
5b	The factory at 58, King Street, Maidenhead, November 11th, 1918.	39
6	Rose Allen and John Benton.	40
7	William Allen, camera maker.	40
8	Chris Jorss, senior.	41
9	J. F. Benton's last patent.	42

Acknowledgements

I am indebted to the "Maidenhead Advertiser" newspaper for their kind permission to reproduce the reports on the "Air Car" and Mr Allen's death and funeral, to the Oxford University Press, Australia for the extracts from the book by Davies and Stanbury:– "The Mechanical Eye in Australia ... Photography, 1841 – 1888", and also to GEC – Marconi for their permission to reproduce the photograph of the wireless operator on the cover of this book.

Introduction

This book is about a German family who emigrated to Australia in the late nineteenth century and it consists mainly of a collection of letters and documents which tell of their happiness and sadness, their successes and their failures in the world of that time.

It also contains the biography of a man who was way ahead of his time and very nearly earned himself a place in the history of aviation in this country.

I would like to thank all those people who helped in the writing of this book, in particular, John Allaway, Michael Bayley, Gordon Cullingham, Mike Goodall, Alan Kempton, Joan Reese (Australia), Michael Starr (Australia), Mrs S Waller and Marlene Wilson (Australia), who gave their time to research the many facts, that, thanks to their efforts, I have been able to include in the story.

Familienforschung Jorss

For all of us who followed them, the account of the Jorss family begins on the 25th November 1831, for it was on that day that Chris Jorss was born in Lubeck, Germany, christened Johann Heinrich Christian Jorss and baptised in the Lutheran faith.

A picture of life in those days can be gleaned from the history books and will almost certainly turn out to be no less dangerous, uncertain and wild than is life today – we know more about what to expect than they did, we have more tools at our command to overcome the trials and tribulations but it is quite certain that we are far more vulnerable than they ever were. Around 1858 young Chris took himself off to Australia, probably in company with a whole group of emigrants, the names Oldorff, Appel and Ebneter occur in the story from time to time and historians tell us that there was a big movement of German settlers to Australia from the late 1840's, many were Government assisted, but many also travelled as paying passengers. Vine dressers were very welcome immigrants at that time.

The date of Chris's arrival in Australia around 1858 came to light from a statement on his death certificate, there is a section headed "Where born and how long in the Australasian Colonies or States", the answers given are "Lubeck, Germany" and "About 46 years in N S Wales". He was naturalised as an Australian at Warwick, Queensland in 1864.

The year 1869 finds Chris back in Lubeck and marrying a girl called Wilhelmina Sophia Catharine Oldorff on the 6th July, it is likely he went back to look for a wife or of course he could well have returned to his childhood sweetheart.

Events now moved at a fast rate, on 23rd July 1871 Baby Anne arrived, christened Anna Agnes Marie, she was destined to have a very interesting and full life, appearing on the stage in America in the 20's as a singer. Next on the 24th November 1872 Baby Christian arrived, he was christened Heinrich Wilhelm Friedrich Christian and he was to lead a steady, satisfying and full life in Australia, turning out to be a popular and likeable chap, very successful in his business as an importer of musical instruments in Queensland.

So that was the Jorss's, Mamma, Pappa and the two babes safely settled in Lubeck until when just two years later Chris decided Germany was no longer the place for him and off he went back to his beloved Australia taking his family with him, never to return until the last years of his life and then only for a brief visit. His wife Wilhelmina did come back after her husband died and spent the last two years in Lubeck before she herself died in 1908.

Back we go now to follow the fortunes of this vigorous young family from Germany in this new land so very different and so far away. There are only some 16 million people in the whole of the vast continent of Australia now and most of those are around the "edges" in the big cities, so it is not difficult to imagine the stark loneliness of the place in 1874, just you and the Aborigines and the heat and the wind and the very occasional rain!

At some point in his life Chris took up the science of photography, he certainly knew about it when he went back to Australia with his family, there are dates in his personal notebook about some photographs that were taken in New Zealand after their arrival in Napier on the "Fritz Reuter", for their ship sailed directly to New Zealand from Hamburg and short account of the voyage will be found in the appendix.

Maybe someone in his family knew about the craft or perhaps he was apprenticed to a photographer either in Lubeck or Hamburg, his personal notebook was bought in Hamburg, those possibilities are sadly lost to us.

Anyway the result of this training was that for the next twenty years or so Chris travelled around the Sydney area taking his photographs, his wife and later his children helping him to earn their living. Since he did such a lot of moving about and since few records were kept in those early days and since his travelling was from township to township in the great Outback of Australia his exact movements are vague in the extreme.

However we come now to the most important event in their lives as far as our story is concerned, on the 26th September 1882 another son was born to them, he was christened in the Lutheran faith: Frederick Franz Johannes, and arrived on this earth in Corowa, N S W and was baptised in Benalla, Victoria on the 5th August 1883 when the family was staying in Benson Street.

This child was to have a most eventful and unusual life, he turned out to be quite brilliant, achieving accomplishments far ahead of his time and impressing all who knew him with his engaging personality and vibrant interest in everything around him.

In his letters to his children in later life Chris mentions that young Johnny (we'll call him that now) attended a school in the Waterloo district of Sydney, nothing is known of the schooling of the two older children or how they occupied their early years, it's reasonable to assume that they too went to school in Sydney.

And so it was, Chris and his wife ran a travelling photographic business in N S W and VIC, in the years 1875 – 1893, they have been traced as having been in Cootamundra on the 27th March 1880 "for a short time", in Corowa in 1882 and at Benson Street, Benalla during the years 1884/5.

A book was written recently in 1986 called "The Mechanical Eye is Australia 1841 – 1888" and Chris Jorss gets a mention in this, an extract is included in the Appendix.

So the years rolled by until 1893 when the most dramatic change of all came to the Jorss's, Chris packed everything up, boarded a ship and brought his whole family to England. He was 62. It would be nice to think that the education and well-being of his children were uppermost in his mind and prompted this major change in their lives. As things turned out he and his wife stayed in London for seven years till around 1899 and then they went back to Australia leaving Anne (who was then Carrie) and her husband Fred and young son Johnny to begin their own very independent lives. When he arrived in London the first thing Chris did was to change their name to Benton, "for family reasons", he said, why he did this we shall never know. Perhaps he thought they would all fit in better with an Anglo-Saxon name! They eventually took up residence at "Victoria Mansions", 137 Victoria Street, S W and are listed at that address for 1897 and 1898. In a legal document dated 1900 and drawn up in Maryborough in Australia, Chris Jorss says he had been in England for seven years prior to 1900, there is no address available before 1896.

He had suffered from asthma for many years and he died on the 19th November 1904 during a particularly severe attack, he and his wife were living at Redfern, Sydney at the time. Wilhelmina went to live with her son Chris and his wife Critia in Maryborough and had a pretty miserable time, having to put up with a severe shortage of money and her daughter-in-law, whom she described as a "Demon of a Woman"! She eventually returned to Lubeck in 1906 and died there in 1908.

Appendix 1

1. Jorss "family tree"
2. C V of Chris Jorss
3. Copy of death certificate of Chris Jorss
4. Note from the archival files in Lubeck
5. Report on the voyage of the "Fritz Reuter", Hamburg to New Zealand, 1874
6. The ticket and health certificates issued to Chris Jorss for his journey
7. A list of photographs taken by Chris Jorss whilst in New Zealand en route to Sydney, Australia
8. A series of letters written by Chris Jorss and his wife to their children Anne and John in 1903/1904
9. A note of rent paid in 1885 and the trace on the chemist's address in London
10. The extract from the book:– "The Mechanical Eye in Australia.", and a copy of the advertisement in the Cootamundra Herald, 1880.
11. The facsimile of the first two pages of Chris Jorss's personal photographic notebook dated 1875 – 1885, with translation

Family Jorss of Lubeck, Germany

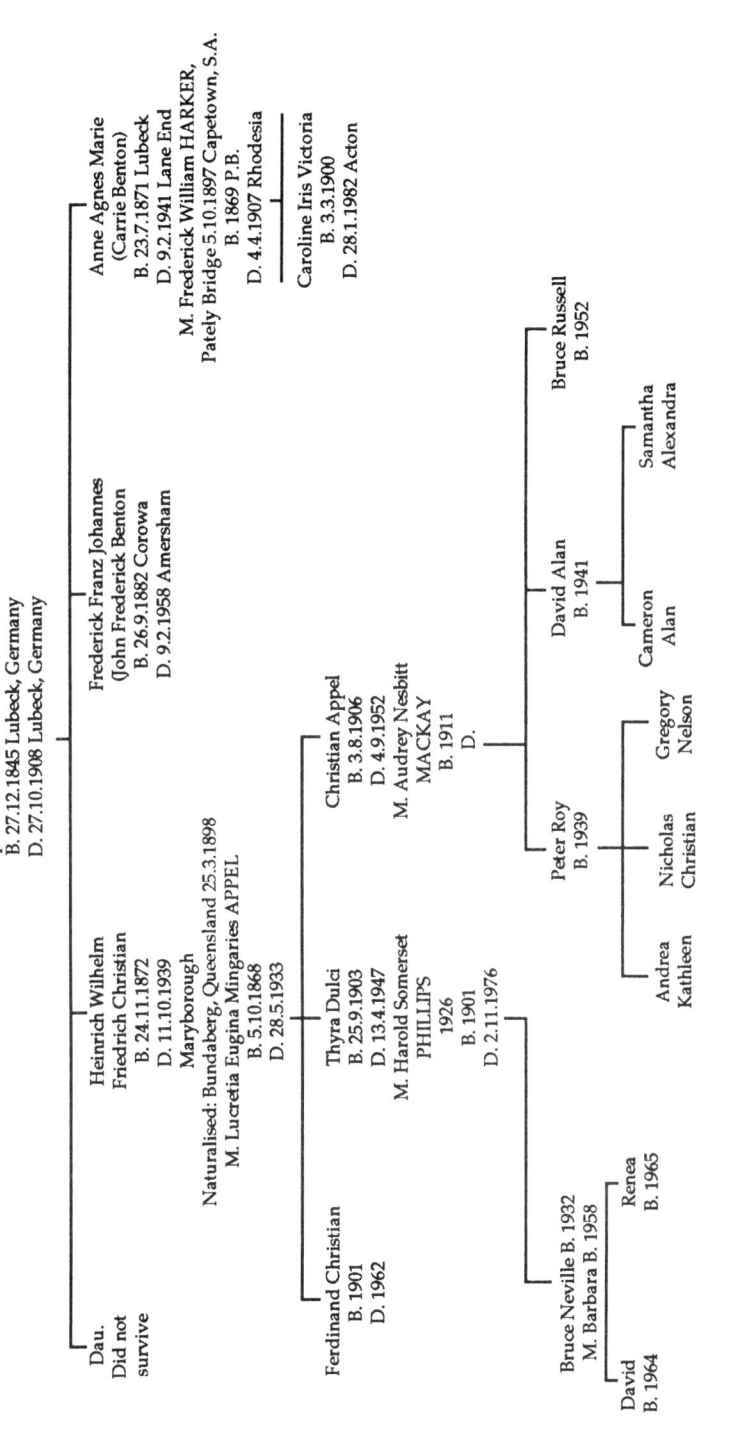

Johann Heinrich Christian Jorss
B. 25/11/1831 Lubeck, Germany
D. 19.9.1904 Sydney, Australia
(Naturalised British Subject: Warwick, Queensland 18.8.1864
M. Wilhelmina Sophia Catharine OLDORFF, of Lubeck on 6.7.1869
B. 27.12.1845 Lubeck, Germany
D. 27.10.1908 Lubeck, Germany

- **Dau.** Did not survive

- **Heinrich Wilhelm Friedrich Christian**
  B. 24.11.1872
  D. 11.10.1939
  Maryborough
  Naturalised: Bundaberg, Queensland 25.3.1898
  M. Lucretia Eugina Mingaries APPEL
  B. 5.10.1868
  D. 28.5.1933

  - **Ferdinand Christian**
    B. 1901
    D. 1962

  - **Thyra Dulci**
    B. 25.9.1903
    D. 13.4.1947
    M. Harold Somerset PHILLIPS
    1926
    B. 1901
    D. 2.11.1976

    - **Bruce Neville** B. 1932
      M. Barbara B. 1958
      - **David** B. 1964
      - **Renea** B. 1965

  - **Christian Appel**
    B. 3.8.1906
    D. 4.9.1952
    M. Audrey Nesbitt MACKAY
    B. 1911
    D.

    - **Peter Roy**
      B. 1939
      - **Andrea Kathleen**
      - **Nicholas Christian**
      - **Gregory Nelson**

    - **David Alan**
      B. 1941
      - **Cameron Alan**
      - **Samantha Alexandra**

    - **Bruce Russell**
      B. 1952

- **Frederick Franz Johannes** (John Frederick Benton)
  B. 26.9.1882 Corowa
  D. 9.2.1958 Amersham

- **Anne Agnes Marie** (Carrie Benton)
  B. 23.7.1871 Lubeck
  D. 9.2.1941 Lane End
  M. Frederick William HARKER,
  Pately Bridge 5.10.1897 Capetown, S.A.
  B. 1869 P.B.
  D. 4.4.1907 Rhodesia

  - **Caroline Iris Victoria**
    B. 3.3.1900
    D. 28.1.1982 Acton

5

Johann Heinrich Christian Jorss

Born:	25th November 1831	Lubeck, Germany
Married:	6th July 1869	Lubeck, Germany
	Wilhelmina Sophia Catharine Oldorff of Lubeck, Germany	
Born:	27th December 1845	Lubeck, Germany
Died:	27th October 1908	Lubeck, Germany
	Naturalised British subject at Warwick, Queensland 18th August 1864	
Died:	19th September 1904 at 17 Crown Street, Sydney, Australia	
Profession:	Photographer	
Death Certificate:	Dated 19th September 1904	
	12009 No 452	
	Application No 1905/2379	

Post Restante Address:
c/o Redfern Post Office, Sydney, New South Wales

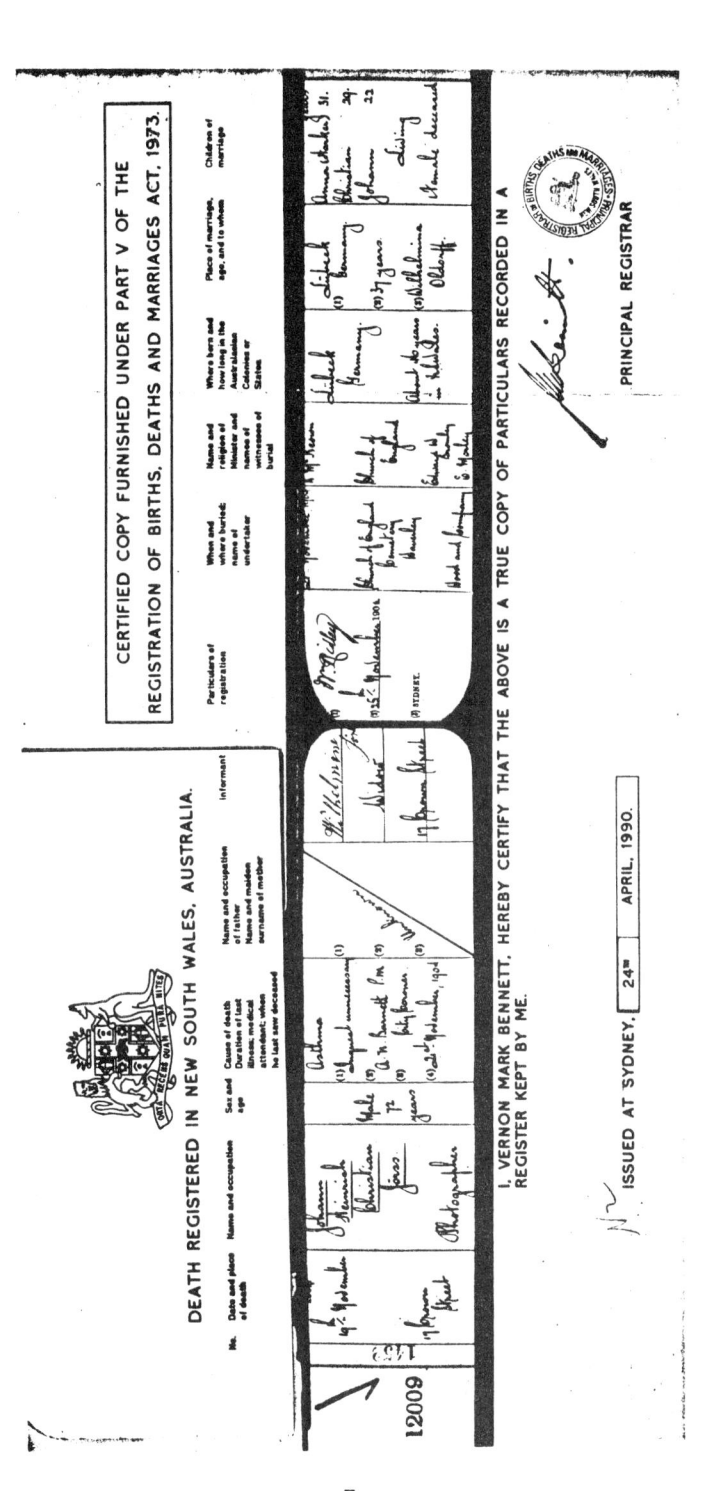

CERTIFIED COPY FURNISHED UNDER PART V OF THE REGISTRATION OF BIRTHS, DEATHS AND MARRIAGES ACT, 1973.

DEATH REGISTERED IN NEW SOUTH WALES, AUSTRALIA.

No.	Date and place of death	Name and occupation	Sex and age	Cause of death Duration of last illness, medical attendant; when he last saw deceased	Name and occupation of father Name and maiden surname of mother	Informant	Particulars of registration	When and where buried, name of undertaker	Name and religion of Minister and names of witnesses of burial	Where born and how long in the Australasian Colonies or States	Place of marriage, age, and to whom	Children of marriage
1453 12009	4½ September 19 Brown Street	Johanna Hannah Bleachan Jones Photographer	Male 72 years	Asthma (1) Chronic exhaustion (2) (3) A.M. Bennett L.m. July Bennett (4) last saw deceased 4th September, 1904	(1) (2) (3)	H. McLaren Mildred 19 Brown Street	(1) J.F. Giley (2) C.E. Melanchthon (3) Sydney	5th September Woodcraft Cemetery Wood and Company	Church of England Emanuel & Martin	4½ Germany about do same in N.S.W.	(1) Sylvak Germany (2) 7 years (3) Philadelphia Oldoff	3 men Charles 39 St. John Johanna 23 Living 1 male deceased

I, VERNON MARK BENNETT, HEREBY CERTIFY THAT THE ABOVE IS A TRUE COPY OF PARTICULARS RECORDED IN A REGISTER KEPT BY ME.

ISSUED AT SYDNEY, 24TH APRIL, 1990.

PRINCIPAL REGISTRAR

Archiv der Hansestadt Lubeck   25th March 1990

Familienforschung Jorss

    The marriage of Johann Heinrich Christian Jorss to Wilhelmina Sophia Catharine Oldorff took place on 6th July 1869 at Lubeck. During the year before the marriage Johann Christian Jorss stayed in Lubeck.
    Wilhelmina Sophia Catharine Jorss died in Lubeck on the 27th October 1908. Their son Heinrich Wilhelm Friedrich Christian Jorss was born on the 24th November 1872 at Lubeck.
    Johann Heinrich Christian Jorss was a photographer by profession. Whether he stayed in Australia before 1868 we were not able to establish here.

No 263   **Berth No**

Hamburg   NEW ZEALAND

That Mr Joh H C Jorss   From: LUBECK
has paid the passage on the lower deck of the sailing ship FRITZ REUTER under
Captain Kolln, sailing on the 20th November from here direct to New Zealand:
for TWO grown–up people,
TWO children,
as noted below, I hereby certify.

Included in the passage is:
  i   Full board on the journey, (all provisions are handed out properly prepared
      and cooked).
  ii Baggage allowance per adult is $^1/_2$ cubic metre, children half that allowance.
  iii Insurance of the baggage to the value of 30 __ per adult, children aged 1 – 12
      half.

Excess baggage is charged with 20 __ per cubic metre ($^1/_2$ __ per cubic foot Hamburg measure). The baggage has to be clearly labelled with the owner's name and each passenger is responsible for his own baggage. The undersigned cannot be held responsible for lost belongings. With regard to the insurance of baggage: in case the baggage is lost because of loss of the ship, the passengers will receive the amount mentioned above after proving entitlement, then adults will receive 30 __ and children between the ages of 1 – 12, 15 __; should part of the baggage be salvaged compensation in part will be paid. The passenger will have to have their loss signed and certified however by either the captain or appropriate local authority or consul. According to orders by authority, insurance is law and by using a most respectable local assurance company it is additionally taken care of, that in case the ship should meet with an accident and it should be unable to finish its journey, the passengers will be taken to their final destination by other ships. Cabin passengers will in that case only be carried to their destination on the lower deck and for that reason have to specially insure the passage fare for the first cabin but have no claim on being carried in the first cabin, even so they are insured for extra passage, and no reimbursement will be made in such case.

Passengers will receive three days of free board and lodging until embarkation, as well as free transport of their person and baggage to board ship, further one mattress, one blanket, two sheets, one water–bottle, one plate, one mug, knife and fork, two spoons and three pounds of soap will be provided, these items will remain the property of the passenger. Even though a blanket is provided it is each passenger's duty to bring along another blanket and feather bed (cover filled with feathers), because this is not only necessary on the journey but very useful in New

Zealand. Passengers of the first cabin have to provide their own bed and bedding and pay for their stay here before, my passengers are allowed to stay on board free of charge for two days after arriving at their destination.

It is the passenger's duty, except for passengers who have paid the full passage, to provide me with a medical certificate that they are physically and mentally fit and have been vaccinated, as well as a character reference on one of my special forms.

Apart from that, my printed conditions come into force, namely that the passengers of the 2nd cabins and the lower deck will in case of late departure of the ship, receive free board and lodgings from the following day until embarkation, or will receive a legally laid-down amount of money for their board of 12 __ for each adult and children between the ages of 1 – 10 years half that amount per day as compensation.

Passengers of the first cabin will receive double the amount of money for their board as compensation, if the voyages should be delayed for more than five days, on no account will a further compensation be paid after that.

The passengers have paid:

a   The ones entitled to a free passage, II __ for adults and 6 __ for children between 1 and 12 years old.

b   full-paying passengers for adults, children, babies

HAMBURG, 1874   C A MATHEI

This is a personal receipt and it should be kept and should be shown on request.

Note: *It is likely that the missing money value sign is a drawing of the £ pound Sterling symbol, this mark will be found in the facsimile of the travel ticket on the next page.*

No. 263
HAMBURG.

Coje No. [handwritten]
NEU-SEELAND

aus [handwritten: Füssen]

Daß Herr [handwritten] die Passage im Zwischendeck des Segelschiffes Fritz Reuter, Capitain Köhn, welches am 20. November von hier direct nach Neu-Seeland expedirt wird, für [handwritten] erwachsene Person [handwritten] Kind

bezahlt hat, bescheinige ich hiermit.

wie unten bemerkt, bezahlt hat, bescheinige ich hiermit.

In der Passage ist inbegriffen: 1) Vollständige Beköstigung während der Reise, (aller Proviant wird gehörig zubereitet und gekocht vertheilt.) 2) ½ Cubic-Meter Frachtgut für Erwachsene, hinter die Hälfte. 3) Versicherung des Gepäcks im Werthe von 30 ℳ für Erwachsene, Kinder von 1 bis 12 Jahren die Hälfte.

Die Ueberfracht nach Neu-Seeland beträgt 20 ℳ pr. Cubic-Meter (¼ pr. Cubic. Hamb. Maaß). Das Gepäck ist mit dem Namen der Eigenthümer zu versehen, und hat jeder Passagier auf das Gepäck selbst zu achten, da der Unternehmer für verloren gehende Effecten nicht verantwortlich ist. Bezüglich der Versicherung des Gepäcks, im Fall für Gepäck durch Verlust des Schiffes total verloren gehen sollte, nach stattgehabtem Beweise von Seiten des Passagiers, zu zahlen den 30 ℳ für Erwachsene und 15 ℳ für Kinder von 1 bis 12 Jahren ausgezahlt, wird ein Theil von dem Gepäck gerettet, so findet die Vergütung theilweise statt. Der Passagier hat jedoch seinen Schaden durch den Capitain, durch die betreffende Ortsbehörde oder durch den Gerichtsstand beim Antritt der Reise feststellen zu lassen. Durch obrigkeitlich rekrutirte Versicherung bei den theils in hiesiger Assecuranz, Compagnie, für versichert gelten, daß, im Fall dem Schiffe ein Unglück zustoßen und es sein Bestimmungsort erreichen sollte, die Passagiere im Zwischendeck nach der Bestimmung gebracht werden sollen. Saludten Passagiere werden in solchen Fällen nur im Zwischendeck und müssen daher das Passagegeld für die Cajüte extra verstatten. Rückzahlung des Passagegeldes findet nicht statt, wenn die Passage auch nicht verschifft ist. Eine jüten-Passagiere werden in solchen Fällen nur im Zwischendeck befrachtet zu werden, wenn die Passage auch erst verschifft ist.

Die Passagiere erhalten bis zum Eintschiffungstag für 3 Tage reichlich Proviant und Beköstigung, sowie freien Transport ihrer Person und des Gepäcks an Bord des Schiffes, ferner 1 Matratze, 1 Decke, 2 Bettlaken, 1 Wassertasche, 1 Teller, 1 Trinkbecher, Messer und Gabel, 2 Köfsel und 3 ⅛ Stangenlicht geliefert. Der Proviant selbst Eigenthum der Passagiere. Eventuelle eine Decke geliefert wird, so muß ich doch in jedem Passagier verstatten nach Betten und Deckbetten mitzunehmen, da solche nicht ganz überflüssig während der Reise nothwendig, sondern auch in Neu-Seeland gut zu gebrauchen sind. Passagiere der I. Cajüte haben für Bett und Bettwäsche, sowie für den hiesigen Reise-Aufenthalt selbst zu sorgen.

Nach Ankunft am Bestimmungsorte ist meinen Passagieren gestattet, sich noch 2 Tage unentgeltlich am Bord des Schiffes aufzuhalten.

Die Passagiere sind, mit Ausnahme der getauften Personen, welche die volle Passage bezahlen, verpflichtet, mir ein ärztliches Attest, daß sie körperlich und geistig gesund sind geimpft sind, sowie ein Neumann-Zeugniß, nach dem von mir dazu ausgegebenen Formular beizubringen.

Im Uebrigen treten meine gedruckten Bedingungen, sowie die Schiffs-Ordnung in Kraft; namentlich werden die Passagiere der 2ten Cajüte und des Zwischendecks bei etwa verlegenem Abgange des Schiffes von hier bis zur Einschiffung frei levirt und, oder durch Zahlung des bezahlten Aufenthalts deren 12 Sgr. für jede erwachsene Person, Kinder von 1 bis 10 Jahren die Hälfte, pr. Tag entschädigt.

Passagiere der ersten Cajüte erhalten doppeltes Reisgeld, wenn die Expedition sich um mehr als fünf Tage verzögert. Eine weitere Entschädigung wird in keinem Falle gewährt.

a) Diejenigen, welche eine freie Reise erhalten, zahlen 11 ℳ für Erwachsene und 6 ℳ für Kinder v. 1 bis 12 Jahr.
b) Bezahlbare Passagiere für [handwritten]

Hamburg, 1874

C. A. MATHEI.

Diese Quittung ist nur personell, muß aufzubewahren und auf Verlangen dem Capitain vorzuzeigen.

C. A. MATHEI Hamburg.

Comptoir: Steinhöft Nro. 8.

Impf-Schein.

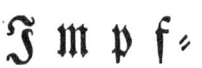

Daß *Johann Heinr. Christ. Jürgs* geboren in *Lübeck* angeblich *2 1/2 Jahr* alt, den *11 Juli* 18*34* von Unterzeichnetem vaccinirt wurde, und daß die Schutzblattern ihren regelmäßigen Verlauf hatten, bescheiniget hiedurch

Lübeck, den *12 Febr* 18*39*

Burck

Health Certificate for John Benton's Father

Impf-Schein.

Daß *Wilhelmine Sophia Catharina Oldörff* geboren in *Lübeck* angeblich *1/2 Jahr* alt, den *19 Jun.* 18*46* von Unterzeichnetem vaccinirt wurde, und daß die Schutzblattern ihren regelmäßigen Verlauf hatten, bescheiniget hiedurch

Lübeck, den *30 Octbr* 18*74*

Burck Dr.

Health Certificate for John Benton's Mother

The following is an account of the voyage of the "Fritz Reuter", the ship the Jorss's took passage on, from Hamburg to Napier, New Zealand, 1874.

It was extracted from the Comber Index which lists all ships which arrived in New Zealand during most of the 19th Century. The Index is held in the Reference Library in Auckland.

The Fritz Reuter sailed from Hamburg on the 28th November 1874, she ran into a storm off Borlaum with the loss of a foreyard and foretopgallant mast. She put into Cuxhaven for repairs and on the 16th December sailed from Cuxhaven.

On the 19th she was through the Downs and on the 29th December at Start Point.

She was at the Equator on 7th January, 22 days from the Elbe. 5th February, Cape of Good Hope, 26 days to Stewart Island (south of the South Island of New Zealand).

8th March off Cape Palliser (near Wellington).

17th March 1875 arrived Napier with 440 immigrants.

"Ship dodging about the bay the last day or so".

28th March sailed from Napier for Callao, Peru.

Tahiti and New Zealand

This document was found in the end pages of old Chris Jorss's photographic notebook:–
1. Port of Papeete at Tahiti, the Society Islands
2. Town of Papeete, Tahiti
3. Diadem of Tahiti with the Protestant Temple in the foreground from Point Venus, Tahiti
4. Rotomahanna or warm lake, hot spring district, North Island, New Zealand
5. Te Tarata, boiling geyser, hot spring district, North Island, New Zealand
6. Tattooed Rock Terrace at Te Tarata, hot spring district, New Zealand
7. Tattooed Rock Basin of Te Tarata, showing Mount Tarawara in the back
8. Herepuru, on the east coast of the North Island of New Zealand
9. Mountain Pass at Honolulu, Oahu
10. Mr Schuler's establishment at Levuhoy, Fiji
11. Pastor Brune's residence at Moorea, the Society Islands
12. Umoreia, Tahiti, an altar where in heathen times the people were burnt by the order of the priests
13. Whahatane, scene of the first massacre of a Government Officer, east coast of New Zealand
14. Lighthouse at Point Venus, Tahiti
15. Catholic Chapel in Moorea, Tahiti
16. Landscape of Oponu Bay, Moorea, Tahiti
17. Oponu Bay and Mr Brune in the foreground
18. The Arsenal in Papeete, Tahiti showing the Chevert in front

Sydney, 18th June 1875
Received from Mr Jorss the sum of £5 Sterling for eighteen negatives with a tongued and grooved box.

Charles Neller

A series of letters written by their parents in Australia to J F Benton and his sister. They cover the period when both of them were in different parts of Africa.

Mr J Benton
c/o Marconi Wireless Telegraph
Station Banana, Congo
Free State, West Africa
                        Sydney, 11th March 1903

Dear Johnny
    Dear Carrie, Fred and Baby have left London on 14th March and have written to us from Naples where they had a good time on their way to Africa. We were very sad as Fred is so unlucky in London and had to go to Africa again to try his luck there. I wish them lots of luck and good health and that we can all meet in London once again. Dear Johnny, I see from Carrie's letter that you have set off for Africa and you will like it there and that you will be lucky and successful in your business and when you get back to London do write to us right away because we are always so glad to get your letters. We got the £4 alright and we thank you very much. Mamma and I are keeping well in Sydney and we had a lot of rain here right across the whole of Australia and the farmers will have a good harvest and everything will be nice and green here. Last summer everything was so dry and very expensive and 10,000 sheep perished here. They couldn't find grass and water and everything was very dry here and very expensive and now everything is cheap again because we have a lot of rain here.
    In Sydney everything is being brightened up, we are going to have a new railway station and it is supposed to be ready in three years time and a new bridge across the harbour to Northshore which is supposed to be ready in six years and will costs £20,000. The bridge will be built so high that ships can pass through underneath.
    The school you went to in Waterloo has been made larger and everything has changed here and the electric train can now reach all the suburbs right through Sydney and so everything is getting more beautiful here.
    Dear Johnny we wish you lots of luck, good health, a long life and thousands of kisses and greetings from dear Mamma and Poppa H Jorss and write to us soon.
    Redfern Post Office, Sydney, Australia (Stay healthy on your journeys)

Sydney, Australia   17th March 1903
                                                    St Patrick's Day

Dear Carrie, Fred, Johnny and Baby

   We received all your letters alright. The one with the two photographs of Baby and £10 and Johnny's letter with £1 and we thank you very much for them. We were so pleased to get the photos of Baby. Baby looks so much like Fred, she must be a beautiful child. We hope that God will look after her health, a pleasant journey to Africa, lots of luck in business and good health.
   At the time, when we set off from Hamburg to Sydney, you were so small, three years old, just as old as Baby is now, three years old. We were very lucky at the time, in the business in Australia and we were always happy and cheerful together and made a lot of money and therefore we hope that Fred will also earn a lot of money in Africa.
   We were very pleased that the received the beautiful things alright, dear Carrie, if the petticoat for Baby is too long, then you can keep it and put it by, it will fit Baby in about two years, and dear Johnny, I am sure, was very pleased about his watch and shoes.
   Dear Carrie, we were very sad to learn that you and Fred wanted to journey to Africa, but Fred must know what is best for him and as he is well known and knows the country he could make his fortune soon, I am sure you will like the climate.
   I had always hoped that we would meet up once again in London, but now we have to wait a little longer until we see each other again, I would have written to you a long time ago, but I didn't know where to write to. We were so pleased to get Johnny's letters, how well he is thought of by the high–up gentlemen and his directors and that he is so good in his business and that he is strong and healthy and that everybody likes him. Johnny will feel strange and odd when you, Fred and Baby have left. He is so attached to you and always knew where to go and he spent so many lovely days with you and always played with Baby, Johnny will never forget all the good things that you and Fred gave him.
   Here in Sydney everything is looking very lovely but shops are having a bad time and lots of people have no money and everything is very expensive because of the high amount of customs and excise; vegetables and meat and fruit are cheaper again here and we are having a lot of rain all over Australia, and farmers are happy. The Government is importing ship–loads of grain from America to share it out between the farmers so they can sow the young crops, because last year we had no harvest at all. We will have a better year then because there is a lot of grass across the whole of Australia and there will be fodder for all the winter for the sheep and a new gold–field has been discovered about 1200 miles from Adelaide. It is supposed to be very rich and many people go there and it is difficult to get there.
   In the last letter I wrote to you I said that I wanted to travel but I didn't make it because I got very bad asthma and could not go out for three weeks. I am quite healthy now and a lot stronger, Christian has sent me three pounds. We took a

cheap flat with good people where we are well off. Mamma and I are quite happy together here and we are hoping for very nice letters from you from Africa regularly and also from Johnny from London.

Johnny goes under the name of Benton, I saw it in the Post Office when I received the £1 in the mail, I will write to Johnny as soon as I get a letter from him, I hope that he is going to stay in England.

We are happy and healthy and wish you a very pleasant and lucky journey and don't let anything happen to Baby.

With lots of luck, good health and a long life from dear Mamma and Poppa, H Jorss

Redfern Post Office, Sydney

With lots of greetings, kisses and a pleasant journey.

We had very bad weather here for four weeks, 100 degrees in the shade and now we will soon have winter and pleasant days.

Mrs C Harker, c/o Mrs Irons   Sydney, 30th March 1903

46 Rollo Street, Battersea Park Road, London

We received your letters and money alright as I told you in my letter before the last. Your letter containing £32 and Johnny's with £4 we received and we would like to thank you very much, and the two pairs of trousers, jacket and waistcoat of dear Fred we received as well and I thank you very much. I made it straight-away to fit me and it suits me wonderfully well, now I have things to wear for about ten years.

I am sorry you went to Africa but Fred must know what is best for him and we will hope that he will do good business and we pray to God every night that He might give you all a safe and happy journey and that you get to Africa fit and well and that you, Fred and Baby will like it there and that Mamma and I will get good letters from you.

Mamma and I are keeping well, we had it very hot for four weeks, 100 degrees in the shade and I got asthma and couldn't go out for three weeks and I had to give up my travels because I felt so low. Then a woman told me to rub myself with olive oil every night from top to toe, I rubbed until my hand was dry and after eight days I felt better and I was able to walk well and that did my whole body a lot of good and made it strong and my eyes are a lot better and clear and got rid of all the blackheads and spots on my face. The ladies use olive oil here to make themselves more beautiful in the face, it gives the girls a lovely skin and takes all the sickness out of the body, should you feel weak and ill, you should try it and it will do you good.

I have not had a letter from dear Johnny for a long time, I hope he will stay in London where he can train and educate himself better. Johnny will not forget the good things he has had from you and we thank you and Fred for your kindness and how welcome you made Johnny in your home and the time he stayed in London with you was good. When Johnny has time he could have his photograph taken and send us the picture, we would be so pleased and were so pleased to get the photos of Baby, it is a beautiful child and we hope she will always be healthy and that she will be big and strong and hope that Johnny will wear his watch and shoes in good weather and that he will be an important man in his business and we wish him lots of luck and a long life and very good health and we hope that we soon get letters from you from Africa and that you, Fred and Baby will arrive there and we wish you all lots of luck and good health and a long life and thousands of kisses and greetings from dear Mamma and Papa H Jorss.

c/o Redfern Post Office Sydney

Mrs C Harker   Sydney, 15th May 1903
Fort Jameson, North Eastern Rhodesia
via Chinde, Africa

Dear Carrie, Fred and Baby

We received your letter from Naples and hope that you enjoyed yourselves on your travels and hope Fred is doing good business in Africa and we received £32 and all the other things and letters alright and we thank you very much. I got the things, the two pairs of trousers, jacket, waist and overcoat from Fred and the blue frock for Mamma, we thank you very much. I got the blue frock ready right away and it suits Mamma very well. I have written to Johnny in Africa to tell him we received the £4 alright and hope that he arrived safe and well and that he is happy in work. I have sent two letters to London, c/o Mrs Irons and asked here to pass the letters onto you, dear Carrie. Dear Carrie we hope you arrived safe and well in Africa and that you all like it there and that you will have a nice house and that bush life will agree with you. You know bush–life from Australia, you lived in the bush a long time and we always felt healthy and earned decent money and I hope that Fred will earn a lot of money and that you will all like it there and Baby will like it there and that she will have a lot of room in the garden where the beautiful flowers grow, to play in and hope that it is a healthy place.

We feel quite well here in Sydney, we have a lot of rain and everything is very green here and we will have a good year and times will be better and farmers will have a good harvest and food is good again here because we have had a lot of rain across the whole of Australia and the climate is pleasant. I hope that everything will be alright again and that we will all see each other again and will be happy together.

We wish you lots of luck, good health and a long life and thousands of kisses and greetings from dear Mamma and Poppa H Jorss.

Sydney, Redfern Post Office
Thousands of greetings to Baby

My Dearest Johnny   **Sydney, 1st June, 1903**

We received your dear letter,
You must be very important in your line of business, I wish you could invent something you would get real money for. The gentlemen must think a lot of you that they have such a lot of confidence and trust in you to send you to Africa. Take great care that you don't suffer from sunstroke and always wear a large hat.

Dear Johnny, I won't let anybody photograph me any more, I am too old and too ugly. Our Carrie and her little daughter must be quite sweet. Try and stay healthy and be careful on your travels. We are keeping quite well but the people here do a lot of slander and lying reports about me just as they did in London. It is very annoying, I wish we had enough money to travel to Germany and could live there in contentment in our old age, Dear Johnny.

How nice that you are learning to speak and write French, it seems you have to speak in French, that is always handy, then you will be able to speak three languages.

We would like so much to live with Carrie in Africa if that could be made possible.

Papa has re-started the matter of his inheritance from his aunt Frine Jorss, deceased. You remember the old aunt in Lubeck. He has put the case into the hands of a lawyer in order to throw the nephew out of the house, because he swindled it away from the old lady, and if we win, we will get a few hundred pounds. I feel very homesick for dear Johnny and dear Carrie.

With thousands of greetings and kisses from your loving Mother.

Write to us soon, I hope Fred will be successful in Africa, Christian does not want to know us any more.

Our Dearest Johnny   **Sydney, 1st June 1903**

We have received your dear letter and that you have arrived safely in Africa, which pleased us very much and that you like it there; we are very well, we sent a letter to you about three weeks ago, Carrie sent us your address from Naples.

I hope Carrie, Fred and Baby will like it there, we were so sad that Fred was so unlucky in England and hope he has more luck in Africa and that we might all see each other again in London some time, what great joy that would bring to all of us. If Carrie should write that we should come to Africa, we would go straight away, because Sydney is very boring for us now, every day the same thing!

Your schools in Waterloo and Redfern I walk by often, they are still the same. We often talk about you and hope you make giant steps forward in your business and that you earn a lot of money.

I had a letter from my niece in Lubeck, Mrs Wiet of Reinfeld near Lubeck, Mrs Wiet found us via Aunty Agnes, Mrs Wiet wrote to London two years ago and her letter was returned to Lubeck. In her letter she wrote that she had spoken to a solicitor about taking court proceedings against Sophie and her husband about the plot of land in Lubeck which belonged to my sister–in–law Frine Jorss and which Sophie and her husband swindled Mrs Jorss out of. As Mrs Wiet and I are the rightful heirs, we want to take Sophie and her husband to court. I have been to see a solicitor and we have asked him to write a letter sealed and signed here at the court. That document I have sent to Mrs Wiet in Lubeck, because without that document she can't do anything, as I am the rightful heir and this whole business should come out alright and Mrs Wiet will win and then we should get another few hundred pounds. The land is worth about £2,000, and as there are several heirs we can expect £500, then we would travel to Germany.

Lots of loving greetings and kisses and wishes for good luck and good health from your dear Poppa and Mamma H Jorss.

Dear Carrie, Fred and Baby　　　　　　　　　　　Sydney, 5th January, 1904

We were very pleased to get your letter and that you are all keeping well. I can imagine how hot it is where you are, we have not had a letter from Johnny, only the one we sent on to you. We feel very sad about Johnny and that we don't get any letters from him, something must have happened to him, because they sent Johnny to such a hot and wild country, we have not had a letter from Johnny in ten months.

Dear Carrie, be good and write to Marconi Wireless Telegraph Co, 18 Finch Lane, Threadneedle Street, London, because they are responsible for Johnny and what happened to him and they will have had some news from him and then we will soon have some news.

Dear Carrie, we have written two long letters to you with lots of news and hope that you have received these two letters.

I have not heard any more about my inheritance in Lubeck, well I don't know whether anything will materialise of this, I don't put too much hope on it happening, if my cousin should win the case she will soon let us know.

Mamma and I have lived in Sydney up to now quite happy and satisfied, but now it is sad out here for us because there is no work here. The photographers here all work with boys and young people, who only get ten shillings a week. They say I am too old, I went to the "Macle" River to do some business and I took beautiful pictures there. You have to work for such a small amount of money that there is nothing left, it is a sad business here. Now I will travel to the "Ritchman" River and try my luck there.

Christian has sent us £5 and his wife had a little girl and they are all well and the two children. Dear Carrie, I hope that you and Fred are making a lot of money that Mamma and I will be comfortable and content again in our old age. I am strong and healthy but Mamma suffered a lot from rheumatism last winter with a lot of pain. We have to be thrifty and look after our money that we don't run out. I would like to stay with you some time to get to know the country and take photographs of how the blacks carry the people in the bush.

How is the little Baby? she must be quite big now and will be a big help to you soon and we will hope that we can all see each other again. Here in Sydney everything is going its usual course, we have nice weather and it is summer.

With lots of luck, good health and a long life, with many greetings and kisses to you all from dear Mamma and Poppa.

Dear Carrie and Poony

I am very sad that I don't get a letter from my Johnny, I still hope to get a letter from my Johnny. How wrong that they have sent him out to wild black French men and the terrible heat, just under the Equator sunshine.

Lots of greetings and kisses from dear Mamma.

Sydney   18th April, 1904

Dear Carrie and Baby

It is such wonderful news to know that Johnny is still alive. We have not had a letter or money from Johnny for twelve months and we are in such a state that we will probably have to go into the poor house because it is so difficult to live with Critia.

As the gentleman writes in his letter he has not had any success yet. Maybe there are electric trees which stops the electricity. You have to write to Johnny about that because he does not know that there are also electric trees and plants in India and Australia, they are in all hot countries. Maybe the electricity strikes there, because he does not want to work but when it is raining the electric trees and plants have no power. I wish the gentlemen would take Johnny away from there and send him back to London.

Dear Carrie,

I hope you are all keeping well; we are quite well but so poor, that is is making us ill.

Lots of greetings and kisses from your loving Mamma.

I hope there is nothing seriously wrong with Johnny's ear. Papa and I have a sad future ahead of us. Each letter from here to Africa takes seven weeks so goodbye.

Sydney   18th April, 1904

Dear Carrie, Fred and Baby

We received two letters from you and all your other letters alright, also your letter from London. We were so happy to find out that Johnny is still alive and I hope that he wrote to you straight away, we have not received a letter from Johnny yet. We are glad that Fred got back home from his travels fit and well and that you are keeping well and that Baby has grown such a joy and is such good company for you, Baby must be a beautiful child, Carrie.

Up to now Mamma and I lived quite comfortably here in Sydney, but it is beginning to look bad for us; we have only £16 left and when that is gone we don't know where we can live. I have written to Christian for some help because we are poor now. Should we go to Christian and Critia plays up again, that should not take long, that we might only be there for six months. When we can't go there we will I have to go into the poor house where it isn't very nice. I hope that Fred and you soon get a lot of money and that you will not forget us. The few years I have left to live I would like to live in peace and quiet. I have not had any letters from Lubeck, it always takes such a long time, maybe my letter got lost. Should I get some money, I would travel to Germany and England and start to heal the people here with my molasses and I would make a lot of money there, because I know how to cure cancer and I could never go back. I went to the Manning Rufer but could not make any money there. There is no money to be made with photography here and I am getting too old in any case.

With thousands and thousands of greetings and kisses for you all, from Mamma and Poppa.

H Jorss's address is always:– c/o Redfern Post Office, Sydney

N.B. The word Rufer is Jorss's interpretation of the word River.

Mrs C Harker   Maryborough
                                                              12th September, 1904
c/o Post Office Fort Jameson

North Eastern Rhodesia

via Salibury, Central Africa

Dear Carrie, Fred and Baby

I received your dear letter from 6th July alright and also the one before. It is a great pleasure for us to get your letters and all your other letters we received alright; the two parcels you sent for Mamma but not the parcel Fred sent for me. It must have got lost in Capetown, because if it had reached Sydney I would have had it, the postman said it can be traced where it was lost, as it was entered in a book. I am very sad about the loss of the parcel, because the two suits of Fred would have helped me a lot, you have to make some enquiries again. Up to now we have not heard anything from Johnny since February 3rd, no 1.8.6. alright, I have also had a letter from Lubeck. My niece Mrs Wiet writes to me that she has been in front of the court with the decorator, he stood there in front of the gentlemen and said that the house had been given to him and he had to swear on oath that it was true but he didn't want to. After that he had to leave the room. And in November the case comes before the court again and Mrs Wiet says he can't swear on oath because he has nothing to show that he was given the house and that she thinks she will win in November because she has a good solicitor and the painter hasn't, so we have to wait to have it assessed.

Christian has been travelling away now for three weeks and you can't live with Critia, she has a new servant each week, they don't stay long because she drives them all crazy. When Christian comes home, I will ask him to give us money that we can go to Sydney because you just can't live with his wife. There are lots of ladies who visit us and who invite Mamma to visit them, but Critia has taken the flowers off Mamma's hat that she can't go out and she thinks bad thoughts against us.

Christian is quite good, if he had a better wife we could live for ever with him. All the people like him and he is good in his business but having this woman he can't get rich, what he realises now.

My address: Redfern Post Office, Sydney

With thousands of greetings and kisses to you all from dear Mamma and Poppa C H Jorss.

And lots of kisses to Baby.

Christian does not know we get letters from you.

Mr Jack Benton

c/o Mrs Irons

46 Rollo Street

Battersea Park Road

London, SW

Maryborough, 1st October, 1904

Dear Jack

We received your dear letter from 11th August, and the enclosed £60 alright and thank you very much, it gave us both such pleasure as we have not had a letter from you for such a long time and that you are back in London now and you can have a look round again in that lovely big city and that Mrs Irons and her family are alright.

We received your letter right on your birthday, and we congratulate you belatedly and that you always stay in very good health and lots of luck in your life and that you always make good progress. Send us your photograph.

We always get letters from Carrie and she always sends us money; Carrie is very good because she never forgets us and she has a good husband and Baby is getting bigger and bigger and she is a great help to Carrie. We have been living with Christian in Queensland now for five months, he is doing well in business. He imports pianos and musical instruments from Germany and sells them here with a large profit. Christian is well liked here because everybody likes him and everybody speaks well of him and we could always live with him. He is very good to us but his wife is so crazy and nobody can live with her. The servant girls don't stay with her and so Mamma has to do all the work in the kitchen. She has two children, the boy is three years old and the girl one and they shout night and day and have just as bad a temper as Critia. It is indescribable how crazy she is and Christian does now realise what he has married and all the people here were amazed that he married the crazy Critia, I don't want to write any more about it. Mamma would like to write but Critia wants to know everything.

I am writing this letter at a hotel, dear Jack, because we got your dear letter with £60 in it, we will go back to Sydney where we can live in contentment and when we always get a little money sent from you and Carrie we can live quite cheaply in Sydney and will never see Critia again and don't have to write to her again. I would like to live in Hamburg best of all where I would like to be for a few years. We are both strong and healthy and we could still take this long sea journey and I will write more to you in my next letter. Thousands of greetings and kisses from your dear Mamma and Poppa, H Jorss, Redfern Post Office, Sydney, Australia.

Frederick John Benton

c/o Mrs Irons

46 Rollo Street

Battersea Park Road

London

Sydney, 28th November, 1904

My Dearest Johnny,

With a sadness in my heart I have to write to you and let you know that our dear Papa (Daddy) passed away on the 19th November. He had to suffer a lot from asthma. I sat with him day and night, I did everything I could for him, Papa was 72 years old when he died and he always suffered a lot from asthma. I sent Carrie and Christian a telegram. The funeral cost me £9, they did the funeral as cheaply as they could for me. Dear Johnny I have banked the money you sent us in my name. I would so much like to live the last years of my life with you dear Johnny and with Carrie if it would be at all possible, with our dear Christian I would like to live too but I can't live with his wife, with him it would be possible but his wife is a Demon of a woman.

Dear Johnny, are you keeping healthy and well? Keep yourself warm. I am quite well, I am sorry I did not write to you straight–away, but I was too upset. I am staying with some kind English people, her name is Mrs Davis. Dearest Johnny, please write to me right away as I am so alone in the world – John would you like the watch on the gold chain of Papa's? I would like to give you one of these things and Christian the other. I intend to sell all Papa's clothes as they are all very good things which he had from Fred. I would like to keep Papa's gold ring for myself. I saw Papa's spirit several times, he looked beautiful and was laughing all over his face. I wish I could be with him. Has Mrs Irons' son ever recovered? Give her my regards.

Greetings and kisses for my beloved Johnny from his sad Mamma.

A document discovered amongst Chris Jorss's papers.

Mr BENSON, Chemist

157a Great Portland Street

London, W

1885:

July 28	1 week rent advance	8 – 0
Aug 3	1 week rent advance	8 – 0
10	1 week rent advance	8 – 0
17	1 week rent advance	8 – 0
24	1 week rent advance	8 – 0
31	1 week rent advance	8 – 0
Sept 7	1 week rent advance	8 – 0
14	1 week rent advance	8 – 0
–	–	–
28	1 week rent advance	8 – 0

The following letter from the Royal Pharmaceutical Society is their reply to a request for a trace on the rent statement from Mr Benson, Chemist.

PATRON: HER MAJESTY THE QUEEN

ROYAL PHARMACEUTICAL SOCIETY OF GREAT BRITAIN

1 LAMBETH HIGH STREET · LONDON SE1 7JN
TELEPHONE: 071-735 9141 · CABLES: BREMRIDGE LONDON SE1 · FAX: 071-735 7629
TELEX: 9312131542 (PS G) · BT GOLD MAILBOX: 72: MAG 10186

JOHN FERGUSON · FRPharmS FPS(NZ) · SECRETARY AND REGISTRAR

I regret that I have not been able to trace any information about the pharmacy at 157a Great Portland Street as the Society's records for this period only deal with the membership and registration of individual pharmaceutical chemists and chemists & druggists and not with premises or businesses. However, I have traced a chemist & druggist named George William Benson whose original date of registration was 15 February 1882 and whose address, in 1885, is given as 157b Great Portland Street. This remained his registered address until his death in 1916.

Museum Curator

A note from Lubeck in answer to a request for information on the movements of the Jorss family after their arrival in England, it is believed they visited Germany for a short while before returning to Australia.

Archiv der Hansestatd Lubeck

Muhlendamm 1 – 3

Lubeck, Germany   11th January, 1991

I am afraid I am unable to give you an answer to your questions about the Jorss family's movements from this end, there is nothing on record here. Johann Heinrich Christian Jorss died in Sydney, Australia. His widow, Wilhelmina Sophia Catharina Jorss ne Oldorff died on 27th October, 1908 in Lubeck, Wakenitzmauer 206, at the home of her sister. It is safe to say that the widow Jorss left Australia after her husband's death to return to her homeland.

The following is an extract from a book called "The Mechanical Eye in Australia, Photography 1841 – 1888".

"C Jorss, opposite Cootamundra Herald Office, Cootamundra, N S W 1880, travelling photographer".
"Christopher Jorss, Benson Street, Benalla, Victoria 1884 – 5".
The address of the Herald Office was:-
217 Parker Street, Cootamundra, Victoria.

The following advertisement is from the Herald, it was inserted by Chris Jorss and it ran from Saturday 27th March 1880 to the 15th May 1880.

[Saturday.] COOTAMUNDRA HERALD. [April 3, 1880.

WHEN!!!

WHEN SPEAKING OF PURCHASING YOU MENTION THE NAME

KIBBY, Cootamundra.

When asked who has the largest stock in Cootamundra the answer select from you

KIBBY, Cootamundra.

When requesting your friends to name the store where to meet them when in town they reply at

KIBBY'S.

When you walk into Kibby's Store, in your front, to your left, and to your right you see nothing but an immense stock, which seems almost like going into a new country.

When you hear people speaking of hard times and see the Wincey's he sells for 3½d. per yard it makes your heart rejoice.

When you see Kibby's full sized Men's Tweed Trouser's for 5/- per pair you feel warmer at once.

When you see Kibby's Blankets at 5/- per pair you have the remedy for your cold without seeing the doctor.

When you see the Prize Medal Prints at Kibby's for 6½d. per yard you will remark they are honestly worth ...

When inquiring where the people of Gollondoon, Jindaloe, Cullinga, Bethungra, Coolac, and Gungagong got their parts as they reply

KIBBY'S, Cootamundra.

Don't be deceived by windy advertisements and high prices, as you can get your goods as cheap as ever at

KIBBY'S.

When asking what causes the Rush at Kibby's, the answer is that he sells a better class of goods for less money than any other House in town.

When you see Kibby's Stock of Clothing you are at once convinced that you are in the right place for New Goods, Good Goods, Stylish Goods, and a good fit.

When and while Kibby regulates the quality and prices for you, you cannot do better than stick

KIBBY.

Now that my little talk is ended, can you question my ability to ...

WHEAT. WHEAT. WHEAT.

THE undersigned are purchasers of the above at highest market prices.

MATTHEWS BROS.,

RAILWAY STORE.

A Five Horse Coach

LEAVES the Booking-office (Albion Hotel) Every Tuesday, Thursday, and Saturday.

For Scrubyard, New Rush, returning on Wednesday, Friday, and Sunday.

Mrs. ANGOVE,
Booking Agent.

Portraits. Portraits. Portraits.

C. JORSS,

PHOTOGRAPHIC ARTIST

(Opposite the Herald office).

BEGS to inform the inhabitants of this community and its neighbourhood of his arrival from Sydney, and that he is prepared to take for a short time correct likenesses, half-dozen 7/6, and solicits the favour of their patronage.

Steam Saw Mills, Junee.

TIMBER! TIMBER! TIMBER!

W. J. MILLER begs to inform the ...

COOTAMUNDRA ASSEMBLY ROOMS.

April 3, SATURDAY NIGHT.

SATURDAY NIGHT, APRIL 3.

Don't Forget.

ONE NIGHT ONLY.

Miss Clara Stephenson's

PREMIER DRAMATIC AND BURLESQUE COMPANY,

Comprising

20 Star Artists.

EAST LYNNE! EAST LYNNE!

MISS Clara Stephenson in her great impersonation of Lady Isabel.

Chris Jorss, Photographer

Chris Jorss was one of a small army of travelling photographers active in southern Australia and Queensland. It is not known when he began his work, he may have started it when he first came out in the 1850's or when he came back to Australia with his family in 1874.

We pick him up busily engaged in the trade from 1875 to 1893; he is known to have worked in Cootamundra, Corowa and Benalla. In later years he based himself in Sydney and travelled out from there, one assumes he did this because it was necessary to send his children to school. The family lived at Redfern and one of the schools Johnny attended was in Waterloo.

To give an idea of the volume of the trade, the people listed below were all active just in the small town of Cootamundra – there were dozens of photographers in Sydney, Melbourne and in all the sizeable towns around the coast.

Albion Photo Co	Cootamundra	NSW	1894 – 5
Australian Elite Photo Co	Cootamundra	NSW	1885
Cadogan (Tronier & Cadogan)	Cootamundra	NSW	1877
W P Cunningham	Cootamundra	NSW	1880
George Bros	Cootamundra	NSW	1888 – 97
Horst of Parker Street	Cootamundra	NSW	1887
Bradford Johns	Cootamundra	NSW	1883 – 85
Johnson of Barker Street	Cootamundra	NSW	1883 – 85
C Jorss opp Herald Office	Cootamundra	NSW	1880
Mc Kilbourne & Co	Cootamundra	NSW	1898
Kirkwood	Cootamundra	NSW	1895 – 97
H Kruger	Cootamundra	NSW	1893
Lemont & Kirkwood	Cootamundra	NSW	1895 – 97
John Nerstad	Cootamundra	NSW	1877
Mr & Mrs Nicholas	Cootamundra	NSW	1877 – 79
George H Nicholas	Cootamundra	NSW	1855 & 1887–98
Morgan O'Flaherty	Cootamundra	NSW	1878
Anders Poulson	Cootamundra	NSW	1895 – 97
P Rogers	Cootamundra	NSW	1877
Alfred Sutch	Cootamundra	NSW	1891
Tronier & Cadogan	Cootamundra	NSW	1877
Wm Tuttle	Cootamundra	NSW	1890
Wood(s), Albion Arcade	Cootamundra	NSW	1882

The most popular photograph taken was the little C D V, thousands of these were made and a good proportion were sent abroad to friends and relatives to give them an idea of how their loved ones far away in Australia were getting on. The photographer would invariably advertise his services on the back of the photograph hoping for repeat trade.

The other great source of income was the studio portrait trade, some of these were quite large in size, the subjects had to be set up and posed and were not allowed to make any movement since the exposure time ran into minutes in the early days!

This all changed dramatically in 1900 with the arrival in Australia of the KODAK, this was a simple snapshot box camera using roll film at 1/6 ($7^1/_2$) a cartridge and selling at just 21/- (£1.05p). They sold in their thousands and the word "camera" was replaced in the language by Kodak, people spoke of taking their "Kodak" when going to the beach or on an outing. The days of the portrait photographer were numbered and only the large businesses in the towns survived. There's usually one to a town in England at the present time but they are fading fast, the coin–in–the–slot passport photo booth has taken over and even major events like weddings are going on to video tape nowadays.

Travelling photographers in Australia fell broadly into two groups, the first of these were the people who travelled alone carrying a considerable amount of equipment using a horse drawn van or buggy or actually going on foot! Others, presumably more affluent, went from township to township renting accommodation in the main streets, advertising in the local papers and doing as much business as they could over a period of a few months at a time. It is believed Chris Jorss used this latter method of trading and specialised in landscape work in the Outback, after his return to Australia in 1900, he tried to get work in the studios in Sydney but came up against the competition of the cheap labour of the young people and had to call it a day. His ill health prevented him from travelling and in fact he only lived for some four years before he died in Sydney in 1904. There follows a series of accounts about photography and travelling photographers in the latter half of the nineteenth century in southern Australia.

Julius Albert Rochlitz, New South Wales, 1861.

"In the morning the cold arouses you quickly from the hard bed ... You give your horse some moist oats, you yourself drink some tea, then you start off by compass, meeting thousands of footprints, but none of them helpful; deep tracks cross your way, the paths of cattle and sheep leading to water, from north to south – they won't help you either. If you see smoke from a peak above the half thousand miles of bush around you, then you will soon run into people or bushfire. If you meet up with a fence, you skirt it until you find a 'slip–panel', you lift all three parts off, enter with your covered wagon, replace the three poles again, and follow the wheeltracks which take you to the inner domains or to a new 'slip–panel'. There you will find two or more roofs, under which they keep the hay etc., around them the three or four drafting yards, leading into each other. Beyond this the homestead, behind it the kitchen etc., perhaps a garden around the homestead, or behind it. I enter, and meeting the first human being, I enquire for the head of the house. He comes out, or asks me in, I tell him what I am after, if he does not want my work, in keeping with the colonial custom, I ask for accommodation for the night, they grant it, this means dinner, bed, breakfast ... next morning I either fit out a small room for my work, and as long as I have work I stay, or inquiring from them in conversation the way ahead, I depart. My reception was always very cordial, and they always said their farewell with more respect and sympathy, than when they greeted the arrival of the stranger. However, from the beginning, they always treated me as a gentleman."

The gelatine dry plate introduced in 1880, was a boon to photographers, enabling them to concentrate on the image.

"Changes in Photography: The substitution of dry sensitive plates for the common wet plates has made great progress during the past year or so; the cumbersome old method of dipping a collodion–covered glass plate into water containing nitrate of silver, then taking the picture before the plate has time to get dry, is becoming obsolete both for indoor and outdoor work. Dry plates, having a sensitiveness equal to or exceeding that of wet plates, are now easily prepared, and their convenience and economy have been fully demonstrated. The travelling photographer no longer needs to load himself down with bottles, liquids, and bath apparatus. He simply provides a few slips of prepared dry glass, with which and a light camera he climbs to the difficult places and secures the views he wants. The gallery artist is no longer obliged to waste his business time in waiting for the preparation and development of wet plates after his customers have come; but he may now both prepare and develop the dry plates out of business hours, and thus attend to two or three times as many sitters as heretofore. These dry plates may be kept on hand ready for use for an indefinite period. At the present time gelatine is the base used as the skin with which to cover these plates. The gelatine is dissolved in warm water, bromide of ammonium is added, and the mixture is digested with heat. A solution of nitrate of silver is then added, and the mass is thoroughly mixed and cooked, being kept at a uniform moderate temperature for four or five days continuously. The mixture is then poured onto the surface of the glass plates, dried in the dark, and the plates are ready for use. Such plates require an exposure of only two or three seconds in the camera in order to take the picture. If greater sensitiveness is wanted, then the gelatine–silver mixture must be kept under heat for seven or eight days instead of four or five. This is a very curious fact. Why the sensitiveness is increased by prolonging the time of cooking has not yet been ascertained. The development of the picture is effected by the use of a solution of pyrogallic acid followed by a solution of ammonia and bromide of potassium. The results produced are said to be in all respects excellent."

About 1885, Edmund Diederich became a travelling photographer, using an unusual horse–drawn studio, the telescoping entrance to the studio could be retracted for transport.

About 1890 he converted the mobile studio to a portable unit. It was taken off the trolley and cut into small sections, and a new roof made with several glass panels to increase the light inside. In the early 1890's this portable studio would have been seen in most of the northern towns of South Australia, including Port Wakefield, Balaklava, Snowtown, Redhill, Port Germein, Appila, Wirrabrar, Booleroo Centre, Georgetown, Melrose and Yongala. In these towns Diederich found a suitable block of land and assembled his studio, which was then tied to the ground with wires. For accommodation he rented a small cottage or took rooms at an hotel or lodging house. When business fell off he hung out his "Last Week" sign, and then hired a waggon and packed his dismantled studio and personal effects aboard. Then with the photographer, his wife and small daughter aboard, the waggon would slowly rumble towards the next township.

Some travelling photographers were based at permanent studios and toured nearby country areas only briefly, probably during periods of business downturn, although better photographers normally provided for those unable to visit the studio.

Some itinerants even went to the trouble of erecting temporary studios in each town, when W R George returned to Bathurst after a year's absence, he erected a temporary wooden structure for a proposed three week's visit. George advertised that his new photographic process was twice as fast as his old one, so that his new studio did not need glass. That was fortunate, because his new studio proved rather flimsy, and was "strewn down the main street" by a "hurricane" soon after it was built!

The Personal Notebook of Chris Jorss

There follow facsimiles of pages 1-2 of Chris Jorss's personal photographic notebook in his own handwriting, containing a total of 38 pages and dated 1875 – 1885.

There is also a translation in the form of brief headings of the material on each page of the book.

Jorss's notebook was found amongst his son Johnny's effects as were all the family papers.

It is a small brown covered book measuring about 7" x 5" and contains 38 pages. Jorss used it to record his photographic methods and formulae and occasionally some personal notes of his work.

The book is now in the Photographic Department of the Macleay Museum at the University of Sydney, Australia.

Contents of Chris Jorss's Notebook

Page 1.	Iodide of Potassium etc
	French/German terms for acids.
	Lists of weights.
2.	Collodium.
	Silver bath, agents.
3.	Strengthening.
4.	Fixing.
4 – 7.	Albumen process.
7.	Silver bath for albumen paper.
7 – 8.	Gold bath for albumen paper.
8 – 10.	How to restore an old silver bath when it is coated with slime.
10 – 14.	Dry plate process.
14 – 17.	How to remove a layer of collodium from the glass.
17 – 18.	How to strengthen negative pictures.
19.	Varnishes.
	A weak/matt varnish for retouching.
20.	Gloss wax for albumen pictures.
21.	A very good alabaster process.
22.	Preparation of normal paper.
23 – 24.	
25.	The best alabaster process.
26 – 27.	On colouring pictures in such a way that they not only resemble but surpass yellow pictures.
28 – 29.	Machine for charging with electricity.
29 – 30.	Igniter.
31.	Galvanic apparatus.
32.	How to restore positive pictures which are burnt.
33 – 34.	Silver solution for galvanic gold plating/gilding.
34 – 35.	Gold plating/gilding.
36 – 38.	Various mixtures and ingredients.

Notes on weights

1 Lb	=	16	Unzun	
1 Unz	=	8	Drachm	Avoirdupois
1 Drame	=	3	Scrupel	
1 Scrupel	=	20	Gran	
1 Drame	=	60	Gran	
1 Unz	=	480	Gran	Troy

The Marconi School of Wireless, Frinton-on-Sea

JFB attended the school at Frinton and worked at Hall Street, Chelmsford.

The Marconi Works at Chelmsford

The 'Air Car' at Chalvey, 1911.

The 'Air Car' at Chalvey, 1911.

J. F. Benton seated in the B.6 at Chalvey

The factory at 58, King Street, Maidenhead, November 11th, 1918.

The factory at 58, King Street, Maidenhead, November 11th, 1918.

Rose Allen and John Benton.

William Allen, camera maker.

Chriss Jorss, Photographer.

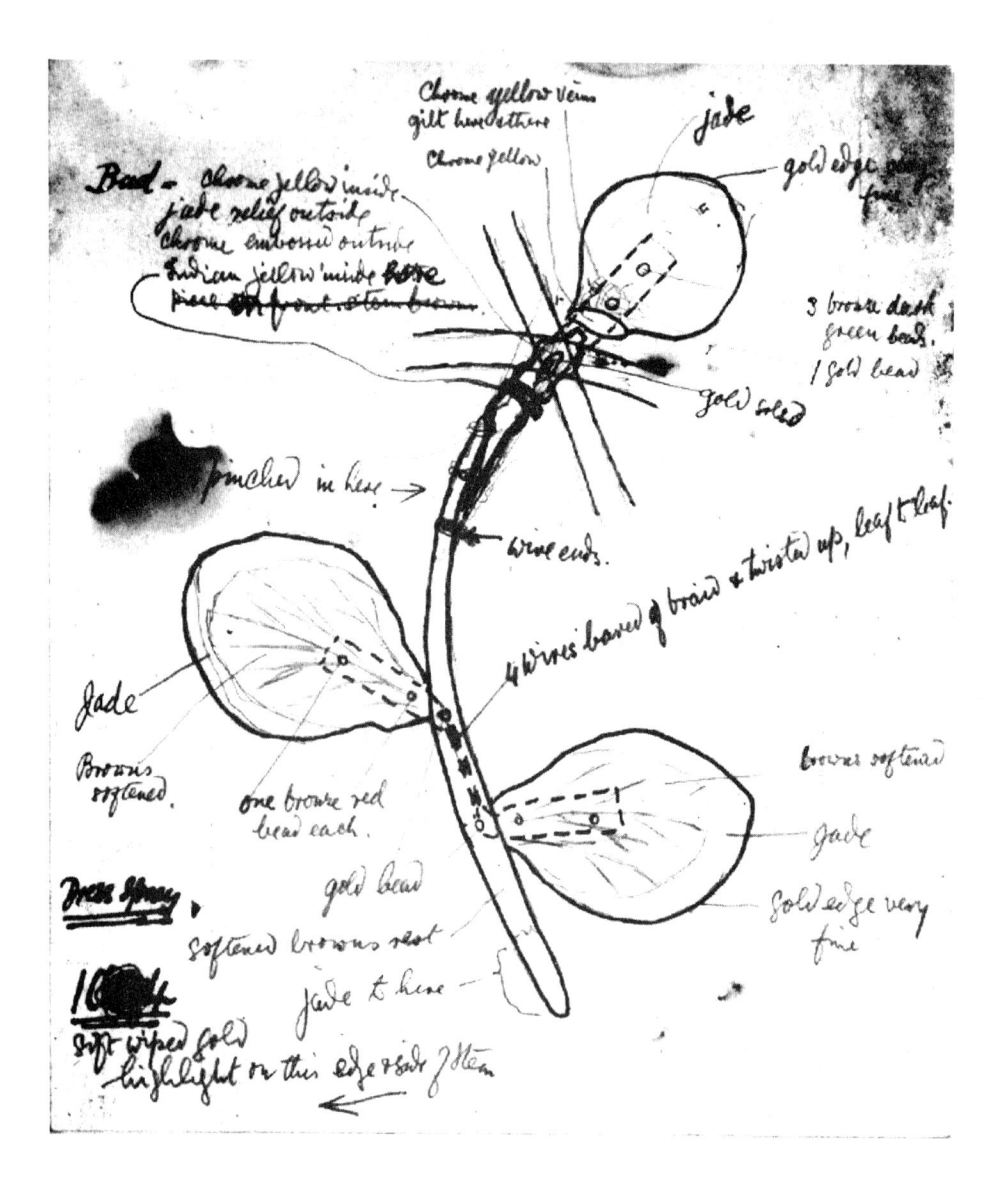

J. F. Benton's last patent.

John Frederick Benton

1882 – 1958
A Biography

Introduction

The door to fame and fortune was very nearly opened for Johnny Benton, in his day there was no State money for innovators and only the rich had any chance of reaching the top, Sopwith began at about the same time as Johnny, with his money he gathered a team about him and his achievements influenced the world right up to the present day.

Johnny lost his partner, had his ideas pirated and was bound hand and foot with red tape, but his spirit carried him along and he enjoyed his life and made the most of every minute, people sought his help and he gave, his presence was an inspiration to all about him: he and his life long companion, the indomitable Sabina Rose Allen, his late partner's wife, were always welcome wherever they went.

Johnny the Flying Man

Johnny had become passionately interested in flying at a very early age and the caretaker of the Mansions at Victoria Street used to give him the staves of old Venetian blinds to make his model aeroplanes, years later Johnny's sister Carrie met this chap on a visit to London and on seeing her his first remark was, "Is your brother flying now?", she replied that in fact he was. Anne married a Frederick William Harker of Pateley Bridge, Yorkshire, in Capetown, South Africa on the 5th October 1897, Fred was employed as a trading agent in South Africa and probably took her out with him. When they were married, Fred insisted that Anne should change her name to Carrie and from that time Johnny's sister was known as Mrs Carrier Harker.

They returned to England and these three young people then set up house at No 4, Wordsworth Mansions, Queens Club Gardens, S W; Carrie and Fred acting as guardians of young John. He attended Westminster City School at 55, Palace Street, S W from 1896 to 1900 where he received an excellent education, he also sang as a boy chorister at the mother church of the school. Johnny was 16 when his parents went back to Australia, his sister 27 and his brother–in–law 30. On 3rd March 1900 baby Caroline Iris Victoria Harker arrived and shortly afterwards the family all moved to No 50, Maury Road, Stoke Newington. John matriculated in 1900 at the City and Guilds College in Exhibition Road, S W, and went on to take a course in Electrical Engineering there and was awarded a First Class Certificate. Helped by a Professor Ayrton he was accepted by the Marconi Wireless Telegraph Company as a student electrician on the 12th March 1902 and was sent for training at Marconi's school at Frinton on Sea, Essex. On the 20th February 1903, he became an Assistant Electrician at Marconi's main works at No 9, Hall Street, Chelmsford and was paid £120 a year at age 21. Then, probably realising the young man's potential, his employers despatched him straightaway to Angola in Africa, in the Belgian Congo (as was in those days) to assist a Lieutenant de Bremaeker to set up a wireless link between Banana and Ambrizette – the two towns were 75 miles apart with a huge mountain between them, so a very tall mast to carry the aerials had to be built, reports put this at 210 feet high, quite a feat in those days!

During his stay in the Congo, Johnny enjoyed a little leave and went up–river to Matadi and on to the Stanley Falls. At Matadi, which means "town of stone" the river narrows down to about 800 feet wide, further up, the width is as much as 14 miles so an enormous volume of water comes hurtling down through the rock gorges and Johnny said that the sight of all that water brought great relief from the blistering heat reflected up from the stone paths one had to walk along.

Bamboo was in abundance in the area and Johnny used to fashion his model experimental aeroplanes using this material, which of course is light and immensely strong.

They had a lot of trouble coping with the weather conditions in the area, these gave rise to static electricity and sometimes they were showered with sparks over an inch long from the apparatus in their huts. Electric light was generated to enable work to proceed after dark and apparently the natives took this in their stride without much surprise at all. The stations were finally finished and working on the 6th February 1904, everyone was very pleased and Johnny returned to England and took up lodgings with a Mrs Irons at No 46 Rollo Street, Battersea Park Road, London, and was there on his own when his mother's letter arrived from Australia telling him of his father's death. By coincidence the Harker family was also in Africa at Fort Jameson, Northern Rhodesia at the time. Carrie had taken the baby out to be with Fred on his trading station, when Carrie returned on her own, she too stayed with Mrs Irons. Johnny carried on working for Marconi's moving around the country helping to put in wireless at various places down in Cornwall and on the Isle of Wight. All the time he was thinking about flying, making plans and models and dreaming about soaring away above the clouds in his very own flying machine. His sister had meantime moved out to Maidenhead with Baby Iris, and Fred was sent abroad again after coming home on leave, by his firm, to Kalomo, Northern Rhodesia, this time on his own. Tragedy then struck, Fred succumbed to the "White Man's Grave", became very ill and died out in Africa on the 4th April 1907, aged just 38, Carrie was 36 and Iris 7.

Carrie fell back on the Harker family for Iris's welfare and a Harker, George Hodgson of Hitchin, looked after her education.

Johnny then moved to Holyport, Maidenhead around 1906 and later he rented a cottage at Pinkney's Green on Maidenhead thicket, it was called Ford Cottage and he lived there for sixteen years from 1911 to 1927. Whilst he was living at Holyport, Johnny met William Allen, these two men immediately took to one another and formed a firm working relationship. Will Allen, a Maidenhead man, was a camera maker of high repute with his business in York Road and his house in Bray Road.

Johnny was inventive, dynamic and had the ability to enthuse all about him with his extrovert personality and drive. When Johnny moved into his cottage on the edge of the common at Pinkney's Green he started work on experiments with kites which he used to elevate wireless receiving aerials, signals and advertisements. Much of this work took place in the middle of the green and he set up a stationary steam engine there attached to a winch which hauled his large man–lifting kite aloft; he devised a reciprocating motion to the cable and this enabled him to make long flights, his record was three hours and he said it would have been much longer had his stomach allowed it! In 1909 aviation received a tremendous boost from Bleriot's cross–channel flight and Johnny's enthusiasm for flying became overwhelming – he influenced Will Allen who gave up his camera business and together they started in aviation in earnest. Johnny rented a 35 acre field at Chalvey near Slough and together they put up a large hangar and began work on building their first aeroplane. They used to cycle over from Maidenhead every day and they also had a small engineering works at Sewage Meadow, Green Lane, Maidenhead; every part of their aeroplane they built by hand, even the two propellors were built up from wooden planks glued together and carved manually. The craft when finished was a large double biplane, powered by a 35 hp. N E C engine driving twin propellors by means of chains. J B patented various parts of his aeroplane – a system for controlling the balance and speed and also a clever sprung undercarriage – he called this machine the B I "Air–Car" and sadly it was not the success they had hoped for, just hopping about the field leaving the ground for only a short while. They set about about improving it and the B 2 appeared, they were so sure of success that they entered this one in the 1911 Daily Mail Circuit of Britain Race, as No 31, but scratched when they found things had once again not gone right! So the B 2 "Air–Car" was dismantled and later Johnny gave the wheels to Sydney Camm of Windsor (the fighter 'plane, Hurricane, designer), they are now in store with the Royal Borough of Windsor collection. Then it was back to the drawing board for the launch of B 3 – this one was completely different with a conventional single propellor pulling the craft instead of pushing it, the water–cooled 35 hp N E C was again used to power the machine and Johnny got it off the ground and made a record flight to the top of Winter Hill at Bisham – a distance of about a mile. Fortune smiled on them and B 4, B 5 and B 6 appeared in quick succession, each mark an improvement on the last. B 6 had a plywood covered fuselage, "Johnny" patented sprung undercarriage and a steerable tail–skid. Other clever refinements included moveable wing–tips which increased the engine rev's aerodynamically and caused the machine to fly faster. Finally there was a B 7, this machine had a reduceable wing, the effective surface area could be reduced by a third whilst flying!

Then came tragedy – whilst trying to start the engine of the aeroplane on his own William Allen was thrown into a corner of the hangar by a back–fire, some little time after this he suffered an aneurysm and died within minutes on the evening of 8th June 1914 at his home at "Bankside".

The following is the Press report of William Allen's death:–

Sudden Death of Mr W Allen 10th June 1914

"The sudden and untimely death of Mr W Allen occurred on Monday 8th of June 1914 at his residence "Bank–side", Bray Road. He was taken ill with haemorrhage about 10 pm and died a few minutes later. Since last Christmas he had trouble with his eyes from which he was recovering and he had hoped shortly to resume his work with Mr J Benton at Chalvey, in the construction of an aeroplane. He was a member of the Primitive Methodist Church for which he was an honest and sincere worker and local preacher. Not infrequently he took part in temperance work. He went about his business no matter whether it was private or for his church and gained the highest esteem of all with whom he came into contact. He was a craftsman who was very ingenious and highly skilled and was interested in all minor work. He followed the occupation of camera maker and had he been possessed of a good amount of capital he would have won fame and fortune by his exceptional gifts and ingenious devices.

During the last few years the deceased was frequently engaged with Mr J Benton, a young Australian, who came to live in Maidenhead, in the work of aeroplane construction in which Mr Allen was deeply interested. The first machine was built in a shed in Green Lane but latterly they moved to Chalvey. In that work Mr Benton has lost an invaluable craftsman and one whom he declares he can never replace."

William Allen's death was a devastating blow to his family, to John Benton, to the local church and to the community. Johnny was utterly downcast and wanted nothing more than to give up the whole enterprise, but Rose Allen, with great determination told him to carry on and a new partnership was formed between them and attention was focussed on the engineering works at Green Lane, Bray Road.

World War I broke out in August 1914, and Johnny then began a long and intensive campaign to sell the designs of the Benton B 6 and B 7 biplanes, this in fact lasted right through the war until 1917. Contact was made with the R F C, R N A S, the French and Russian Governments, and on 25th June 1915, Johnny wrote to Lloyd George, telling of his seven year's practical experience in building and flying his own machines and that he was anxious to show his sixth aeroplane at Chalvey to a Government representative. Lloyd George passed the letter to the War Office who arranged for a Captain Hooper and a lieutenant to inspect the machine on 5th August 1915.

Captain Hooper expressed interest in the B 6, took dimensions and was given descriptive matter and copies of patents. He asked for drawings to be sent urgently to him at the Officer's Mess, Farnborough. On August 17th, John Benton received a letter from Department M A 3 at the War Office refusing to avail themselves of the machine and giving no reasons. Feeling that the War Office had not fully appreciated the capabilities of his 'plane, Johnny visited them and persuaded them to consider the matter further. In addition he obtained the offer, from a Captain Clarke, of a 100 hp engine on loan so that stronger powered trials could take place. On 13th September a further letter was received from M A 3 saying that they did not wish to proceed further in the matter. By the same post a letter came from Major–General Hickman referring to the description and drawings received by his department (Inventions) and saying that they would be pleased to view the machine when it is in flying condition. Johnny replied that as soon as the 100 hp engine arrived, he would gladly show his aeroplane to General Hickman's department. Squadron Commander Babington also visited Chalvey on 13th August on behalf of the Admiralty Air Department, he reported that the B 6 was amateur built, well made, but that it was unlikely to be of use to the R N A S.

On 8th October, Johnny was told by a well–informed friend in the aircraft industry that the Royal Aircraft factory was experimenting on their own account with a machine built to J B's designs but without much success due to lack of data. Subsequently another friend told him that his firm (Whiteheads) among others was making 600 sets of wings for their biplanes to Johnny's design. He was also informed that the under-carriage of his machine had been adapted for seaplanes and was being manufactured for the Government.

Early in October 1915, the B 6 was inspected by an engineering expert who sent details to Professor Hopkinson of the Admiralty Board of Inventions and an interview was arranged with J B for 8th November. Here he gave them full details and plans of his machine together with his new ideas for variable area wings, Professor Hopkinson said he would send them to Mervyn O'Gorman at the R A F at Farnborough for evaluation. When Johnny told his engineering friend what had occurred, the friend wrote, "I am sorry to hear that your new designs are going to the R A F because that simply means that you are liable to the same treatment that other people have to suffer which, judging from previous experiences, seems to be that an idea is studied carefully by the people there, anything original is noted for further use and the inventor is simply told that his idea is impracticable, or at any rate that it cannot be used; then some months later the factory (Farnborough) itself comes out with the same idea and takes the credit for itself". After considerable correspondence, the Aeroplane and Sub-Committee of the Board of Inventions advised J B on the 24th February 1916 that they would not recommend his design for adoption or experiment and that a system for altering the area of the wings of an aeroplane was not of sufficient value to justify the complicated mechanism and additional weight that would be entailed by its adoption.

Johnny continued his efforts to sell his aircraft design – it was shown to Major Wood and Captain Acland of Vickers Maxim, at Crayford who seemed interested, but only if Johnny would allow Vickers to build a prototype at his own expense. As late as May 1916 a Lieutenant A P Thurston visited Chalvey to inspect the modified B 6 biplane on behalf of the War Office. The B 6 biplane remained in the hangar at Chalvey until 1919, when it was scrapped. The hangar was used by the farmer who got his pilot's licence and first kept a D H Moth and then a Monospar there. Some months after William Allen's death John became thoroughly disillusioned and despaired of ever getting a contract and in 1915 almost joined the army; again Mrs Allen stepped in and looked around for work for the firm – it so happened that a bottleneck had occurred in the production of artillery shells due to a lack of containers used in the manufacture of the fuses. They set to work and soon produced tubes made of waxed paper, Johnny took these to the War Office, left them for "consideration" and returned home, time went by with no improvement in the shell supply situation, so Johnny paid a second visit to Whitehall. The story is that the samples were still lying on a table where Johnny had left them; this time he was told that "formers" would be sent to his works and then he could then start production. Back in Maidenhead Mrs Allen felt that more time would be wasted so she went down to Timberlakes Cycle Works and got a length of cycle tandem-frame tubing which was exactly the diameter of the inside of the required paper containers. This was cut up into small lengths – production started and the first batch despatched by return when the order from the War Office was received – they were promptly sent back to Maidenhead with a letter saying that since the formers had not been sent they could not be correct! The W O formers duly arrived, they were of course exactly the same size as the cycle tubing, the same containers were re-despatched to the filling factory and soon after a letter of congratulation arrived on such prompt delivery! After this hiccup, Johnny and Rose Allen set up a new factory at No 58 King Street, Maidenhead, employing some 80 staff, there they made a range of timers for rifle grenades and 18 pounder shells, and also cartons of anti-lice powder for the men in the trenches.

At the end of the War and with the cancellation of the contracts, King Street was closed and Johnny was now finished with flying and the war – he tried making novelty costume jewellery from fish bones and won a lovely Clyno motorcar which was offered as a prize on the purchase of Sunlight Soap with coupons – he bought a large quantity of the soap from a wholesaler, converted the whole lot into soap flakes and sold them all back to the wholesaler! Sunlight got his coupons and gave Johnny the car!

About 1920 he embarked on the "Good Life", reared goats and chickens and became self-sufficient for food – he later purchased a cottage and land at Lane End, West Wycombe and he and Rose Allen ran a large garden, in fact a small-holding tucked away in the glorious Buckinghamshire countryside.

During World War II he was again able to bring his intellect to bear on a most desperate problem – the enemy was dropping "magnetic mines" by parachute as well as the normal sowing in the sea – Johnny suggested that a low voltage heavy current be passed around the hulls of all ships by means of electric cables to "de-Gauss" them. This rendered the ships immune to the mines which did not explode since the electric field around each ship cancelled out the magnetic "trigger" in the mine. He enlisted the help of his solicitor, Captain Frank Medlicott to get this one into the minds of their Lordships in the Admiralty. He and others with this idea saved hundreds of lives in the war at sea.

Turning to his character, Johnny has been described as dramatic, extravagant, inventive and stimulating, a quite remarkable man. His family was theatrical, his sister Carrie became an actress and she and her daughter Iris, whom she affectionately called Poon, went to America in the early 20's and toured around visiting Los Angeles and New York. Whilst in Los Angeles the two girls met a Mrs Eleanor Godwin and stayed with her and her husband Chas, the Godwins persuaded Carrie to speculate on the oil boom current at that time. Eleanor bought the lease on five acres of land at Torrance, California using £1,000 of Iris's money. Her brother Johnny in England supervised this transaction and their business generally, whether any oil money actually came their way is not known but considerable profit was certainly made on the subsequent sale of the lease to an oil company.

John was keenly interested in amateur dramatics and in the late twenties he took the part of Nankie Pooh in the Mikado, staged by the leading amateur society in Maidenhead at that time, he kept his costume and "props" in his personal effects until his death. One of Rose Allen's daughters Rose was an amateur singer and was in the cast with him. Later in his life he became a spiritualist and practised faith healing in Reading using hypnosis, he was always reticent about the results he achieved, he "treated" a considerable number of people sick with a wide range of complaints. John made money on the Stock Exchange by skilful investment, he had success with Japanese stocks in particular, Japan was flooding European markets during the early 30's, all their products were considered rubbish but they sold in their millions, and at the time of writing, Japan is the leading trading nation in the world and their electronic goods are unsurpassed in regard to quality and reliability. Among his many acquaintances John enjoyed the friendship of the Member of Parliament for Norfolk, Mr, later Sir, Frank Medlicott and his family; he also knew the Powles family, their daughter Jean was painting during the early 50's and made a picture of the house and garden at Lane End.

From time to time Rose Allen and Johnny entertained relatives of the Allen family at "Philberds" and Johnny was always a most charming and energetic host, taking the children on country walks and showing them his "magic" as he called it, hiding sixpences in "fairy hideaways" for the children to find. Grandma Rose Allen and he gave splendid country holidays to many appreciative people over the years and around 1931 his nephew Chris, his brother's boy, came over from Maryborough, Australia to stay for a while and Johnny helped the boy to start his career in life. Johnny loved to be spoilt and much enjoyed receiving presents, his extrovert nature embraced all about him in his thoughts and activities, his eccentricities included a keen interest in flags, he put up a mast at Lane End and Rose Allen helped him make the most carefully fabricated silk Union Jacks which he raised and lowered at precisely the right times of day. They set up a croquet course on the main lawn and gave tea parties in their lovely country garden, Rose was always fond of cats and actually trained one to retrieve a small potato which she rolled down a long passage. In the early days at "Philberds" there was no mains water, drainage or electricity and the cooking was done by oil burning stoves, the extended cottage and garden were freehold. The house was approached by a long lane off the road and down by the side of the garden and this was always full of pot-holes, and so to preserve the springs of the car, on arrival home, everyone was made to "de-bus" and walk the rest of the way whilst Johnny drove the car along the drive and into the garage. The extensive gardens produced honey from ten or so bee-hives (Johnny used to lecture on bee keeping), much fruit, apples, pears, currants, many flowers and vegetables, most of which were sold in the village, a dear old man called Twitchen came to help with the garden and his daughter also helped in the house.

To visit Lane End was an experience that remained in one's memory always, the house, the garden, the beautiful countryside and of course Grandma Allen and Uncle Johnny. It all came together to create a haven of peaceful tranquillity far removed from the outside world of frantic trouble and strife, they made their own bit of Heaven at "Philberds". The closing years of John's life were just as dramatic and unusual as the preceding ones, he never married and he became sympathetic towards another man who was "down on his luck", Johnny gave him solace and money in the form of cheques.

In the last years of his life Johnny began to suffer bouts of depression which became more and more severe, not for him our present-day psychiatric and drug therapy, he was living just a little too soon for all that.

The end came as a mental breakdown, John was admitted to Amersham hospital and died there quite alone, his mind closed to the outside world and to all those who knew him.

R.I.P.

Funeral of Late Mr W Allen

The funeral of the late Mr W Allen of "Bankside", Bray Road, Maidenhead, who died under the tragic circumstances reported in our last issue, took place on Friday afternoon the 12th June 1914. The cortege left the house at two o'clock, and wended its way to the Primitive Methodist Church, Queen Street, where a service was held and conducted by the Rev W Shaw, Supt Minister. The service, which was deeply impressive, was attended by a large number of persons. "Am I a soldier of the cross?" and "We may not climb the heavenly steps", two of the deceased's favourite hymns, were sung. There was a large gathering at the Cemetery to witness the last sad rites at the graveside. Quite a touching incident was the singing of the hymn "Rock of Ages" to the old Methodist tune of Eglon. The ceremony concluded with prayer led by the Rev W Shaw. The chief mourners were: Mrs Allen (widow), the Misses Rose, Daisy and Ivy Allen (daughters), Mr Wm Allen (son), Mr Thomas Allen (brother), Mr W Keyte (step-brother), Mr T Miskin (father-in-law), Mr G Keyte (step-father), Mr T Allen, Mr W Keyte, Mr C Miskin, Mr and Mrs Courtney, Mr P Keyte and Mr J F Benton.

The bearers were: Messrs W Folley, A Oram, W Carter and C Wilkins, local preachers and workers. Mr E Carter, Sunday School Superintendent, represented the Sunday School in which the deceased was a teacher.

Floral tributes were placed on the grave from: Mrs Allen (widow), the Misses Rose, Daisy and Ivy Allen (daughters); Mr William Allen (son); Tom and Esther (West Ealing); Mr J F Benton; Mr Keyte (step-father); Walter and Annie and family; Bert and Queenie (Dartford); Daisy, Charlie and Mr Benton; Dan and Ned; Daisy's Will; Nellie and Ernest; Mr and Mrs Howell (London); Mr and Mrs John Castell; "From the Local Preachers and Friends of the Primitive Methodist Society"; "From the Teachers and Scholars of the Primitive Methodist Sunday School"; "From Members of the Press Forward Lodge I.O.G.T."; Mr Leaver and family, High Town Road; "From the members of the Grand United Order of Oddfellows"; "From Friends at 35 Norfolk Road"; "From Mrs Spackman and family, Manor Farm, Chalvey"; Horace, Arthur and Violet, (nephews and nieces); Eva, Mamie and Bernard (nephews and nieces), Mrs Harker, Miss Ethel Fifield and Mr Rock, Mr and Mrs Baker and family, Mrs Watkins, Miss Bennet, Ivy Woodhouse, Rosie Bannister and Violet Baker.

Memorial Service

A memorial service was held in the Primitive Methodist Chapel on Sunday evening in relation to the late Mr William Allen. The family and a large number of friends, including a number of the Good Templars of Maidenhead gathered to show their sympathy with the bereaved family and their appreciation of the deceased. The service was conducted by the Pastor, Rev W Shaw. Mr Alfred Oram, of Marlow, gave interesting reminiscences of his companionship from his earliest years with the departed. The opening prayer was offered by Mr Blumfield. The hymns, "Thou knowest, Lord, the weariness and sorrow" and "Jesus lives, no longer can thy terrors, death, appal us", and the anthem, "The Lord is my Shepherd", were sung. A suitable address, based on the words "He was a good man" were given by Mr Shaw, who also read the following paragraphs after the sermon:-

Mr W Allen was a native of Maidenhead, born in 1861. When only two years of age he lost his father through death by accident. Some six years afterwards his mother was married to Mr George Keyte, who only five weeks ago was called to part with the devoted woman who had shared his joys and sorrows for forty-five years. He is with us today. In the late Mrs Keyte, Mr Allen had a most God fearing mother, whose delight it was to know that her children were serving the Lord Jesus. She led them to the House of God in early life and entered them as scholars in the Sunday School at the earliest moment.

Mr Jessie Wilkins was the Sunday School teacher who most influenced the life of young Allen, and was often accompanied by the boy to his appointments as a local preacher. The friendship then formed and the influence then exercised affected the life of the youth permanently and beneficially. It was during the early eighties, in connection with the Blue Ribbon Movement and a mission held by two of the late C H Spurgeon's students, Messrs Fullarton and Smith, that Mr Allen was led to realise his need of pardon and peace with God. These blessings he received after one of the mission services, but in the quiet seclusion of his own home. After conversion he became an earnest Christian worker. He was greatly interested in the Blue Ribbon Mission work and also in the Band of Hope agency. He also became a member of the local Good Templar Lodge. His temperance work was the outcome of deep rooted principle. The presence of so many of his brother Templars at his funeral service bespoke the esteem they felt for a "brother beloved" and was highly appreciated by the family and church. As a Sunday School worker and officer he held an honourable position for fully thirty years and in his removal the church and school suffer loss.

As a preacher he was quite up to or even above the average. His sermons were the outcome of careful preparation and his message met with considerable success. He had the gift to be coveted, viz, that of gripping and holding the attention of the working man.

He was deeply interested in evangelistic work and some few years ago organised the Midnight Mission, which was so remarkably successful.

As a parent he exercised a salutary influence over the home life and has left a family, all of whom are worshipping with us and engaged in Sunday School or some other kind of work. His children "Rise up and call him blessed".

Those with whom he was brought into daily contact at his employment have the highest regard for him and gratefully acknowledge his gracious and kindly influence over them. A man of moral honour and active goodness he won his way to the hearts of those who were most often in his company, ever acting as a wise and tender parent to his juniors.

His influence has coloured and possibly given character to another life and the word of St John seems to have a peculiar significance to our brother when he writes "Blessed are the dead which die in the Lord from henceforth: yea, saith the spirit, that they may rest from their labours; and their works do follow them".

The Maidenhead Advertiser. Wednesday 24th June 1914

Appendix 2

1. The identity papers of John Frederick Benton, including his death certificate.
2. The two wills of John Benton.
3. Papers relating to J Benton's schooling in Australia.
4. Papers relating to J Benton's schooling in England.
5. Papers relating to J Benton's career with Marconi and his trip to Angola.
6. Some recent letters written by people who knew John Benton.
7. A collection of documents relating to the flying field at Chalvey, Slough.
8. The Press report on the "Air Car".
9. Descriptions of the aeroplanes built by Benton and Allen.
10. A list of Patents taken out by Benton.
11. A series of letters dated 1915 – 1916, relating to the efforts made by John Benton to sell his ideas and aeroplanes to various military bodies. The letters also include some personal ones to his friends who helped him in his work.
12. Newspaper announcement of Admiralty Inventions Board.

Certificate of Baptism

Australia, 5th September 1883.
Benalla, Victoria.
Extract from the register of birth and baptism of the Lutheran faith.
Born on the 26th of September anno domini 1882 in the town Corowa, N S W and baptised in the town of Benalla, Victoria on the 5th August 1883, the father Johan Heinrich Christian JORSS, the mother Wilhelmina Sophie Catharine nee Oldorff from Lubeck, Germany, their legitimate son FREDERICK FRANZ JOHANNES JORSS.
Witnesses: Frederick Oldorff, Lubeck, Germany
         Franz Oldorff, Lubeck, Germany
         Johannes Jorss, Lubeck, Germany
Herewith certified by Jorss a wife.

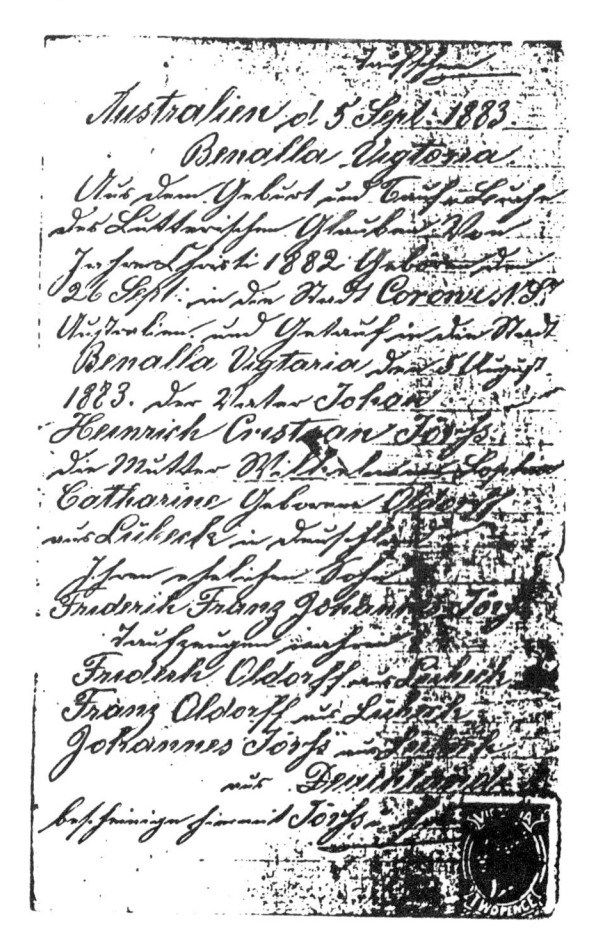

PR220

Application 306085/91/CD

NEW SOUTH WALES

Registration of Births, Deaths and Marriages Act, 1973

RESULT OF SEARCH

I hereby certify that search has been made in the Records kept by me but no trace can be found of the registration from 1880 to 1884 inclusive of the birth of Frederick Franz Johannes Jorss, said to have been born in Corowa, N.S.W., on the 26th September, 1882.

Issued at Sydney, on 20th March, 1991

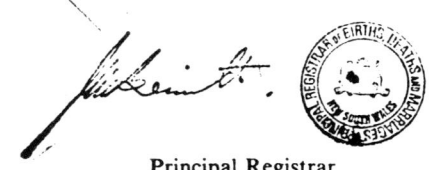

Principal Registrar

S.O. 3145

Dated 26th March 1900
Re JOHN FREDERICK JORSS otherwise JOHN FREDERICK BENTON
DECLARATION OF IDENTITY AND OF AGE

T MORTON
Notary Public
Maryborough
Queensland

A copy of the first page of a sworn declaration by Chris Jorss and dated 26th. March 1900:

I JOHANN HEINRICH CHRISTIAN JORSS of Maryborough in the Colony of Queensland Gentleman do solemnly and sincerely declare -----

1) THAT I was married on the Sixth day of July one thousand eight hundred and sixty nine at Lubeck Germany to Wilhelmine Sophia Catherine Oldorff of Lubeck aforesaid Spinster ----

2) MY SAID wife and I subsequently came out to Australia and on the Twenty sixth day of September One thousand eight hundred and eighty two at Corowa in the Colony of New South Wales my said wife bore me a son who was named "John Frederick" but the birth of the said John Frederick was through negligence never registered.

3) ABOUT seven years ago I together with my family left the said Colony of New South Wales and went to London and resided in London aforesaid for about four years of my said residence there at 137 Victoria Street ---

4) WHILST in London as aforesaid for certain family reasons I assumed the surname of Benton instead of my surname of Jorss and I was always whilst residing in London as aforesaid known by the surname of "Benton" and my children including the said John Fredrick also assumed the said surname of Benton and were known by that name ---

5   JOHN FREDRICK BENTON now residing with my sister Anna Agnes Maria Harker wife of Frederick William Harker of Four Wordsworth Mansions Queens Club Gar ns Gardens London is the same person heretofore referred to as being my son and who was born on the twenty sixth day of September One thousand eight hundred and eighty two at Corowa in the Colony of New South Wales aforesaid ———

AND I make this solemn declaration conscientiously believing the same to be true and by virtue of the provisions of The Oaths Act of 1867 ———

MADE and SUBSCRIBED by the said Declarant at Maryborough in the Colony of Queensland the *twenty sixth* day of *March* 1900 ———

Johan Heinrich Christian Jöss.

Before me

M Morton
Notary Public
Maryborough Queensland
Australia –

TO ALL TO WHOM THESE PRESENTS SHALL COME I
T H O M A S M O R T O N Notary Public duly authorised
admitted and sworn and practising in Maryborough in the
Colony of Queensland Australia DO HEREBY CERTIFY that
JOHANN HEINRICH CHRISTIAN JÖRSS the person named in the
paper writing or declaration hereunto annexed did duly
and solemnly declare to the truth thereof before me on
the day of the date thereof and that the name -- --- -
"*Johann Heinrich Christian Jörss*" thereto
subscribed is of the proper handwriting of Johann
Heinrich Christian Jörss ——————————

    IN TESTIMONY WHEREOF I have hereunto subscribed
my name and affixed my seal of office this *Twenty sixth*
day of *March* in the year of our Lord one
thousand nine hundred ——————————

T. Morton

NOTARY PUBLIC

Maryborough, Queensland.

CERTIFIED COPY OF AN ENTRY OF DEATH

GIVEN AT THE GENERAL REGISTER OFFICE, LONDON

Application Number PAS 367263/90

REGISTRATION DISTRICT Amersham

1958. DEATH in the Sub-district of Amersham in the county of Buckingham

No	When and Where died	Name and surname	Sex	Age	Occupation	Cause of death	Signature, description and residence of informant	When registered	Signature of registrar
356	Ninth February, 1958. General Hospital, Amersham.	JOHN FREDERICK BENTON	Male	75 Years	of Philbirds, Lane End, High Wycombe. of Independent Means.	I.(a) Broncho pneumonia. Certified by E.C.Foot,M.B.	Alan Kempton, Causing the body to be cremated. 151,Grenfell Road, Maidenhead, Berks.	Eleventh February, 1958.	W.E.Stokes Registrar

CERTIFIED to be a true copy of an entry in the certified copy of a Register of Deaths in the District above mentioned
Given at the GENERAL REGISTER OFFICE, LONDON, under the Seal of the said Office, the 27th day of September 19 90.

This certificate is issued in pursuance of the Births and Deaths Registration Act 1953. Section 34 provides that any certified copy of an entry purporting to be sealed or stamped with the seal of the General Register Office shall be received as evidence of the birth or death to which it relates without any further or other proof of the entry, and no certified copy purporting to have been given in the said Office shall be of any force or effect unless it is sealed or stamped as aforesaid.

CAUTION:—It is an offence to falsify a certificate or to make or knowingly use a false certificate or a copy of a false certificate intending it to be accepted as genuine to the prejudice of any person, or to possess a certificate knowing it to be false without lawful authority.

DX 518075

Will

John Frederick Benton 1882 – 1958
"Philberds", Lane End, High Wycombe, Bucks
Died on 9th February 1958 at Amersham Hospital
Death Certificate 6a 311.

This is the Last Will and Testament

of me John Frederick Benton, Electrical Engineer of Ford Cottage, Pinkney's Green, Maidenhead in the County of Berkshire made this Sixth day of September in the year of our Lord One thousand nine hundred and eleven.

I hereby revoke all Wills made by me at any time heretofore. I appoint my sister Carrie Harker and William Allen of 31 York Road, Maidenhead, Berkshire, camera maker, to be my Executors, and direct that all my debts and funeral expenses shall be paid as soon as conveniently may be after my decease.

I give and bequeath unto William Allen, Camera maker, 31 York Road, Maidenhead, Berkshire, my "Swift" bicycle and my share of our British Patent No 9004, dated 4th April 1910 for "elevating carrier for kite or other strings". I hereby appoint the said William Allen to be Managing Director of my Aeroplane Works, consisting at this date of a corrugated iron shed, situated at Green Lane, Maidenhead, Berkshire and an aeroplane shed at Chalvey near Slough, and of the profits from which 70% is to be placed to the account of my sister Carrie Harker of Maidenhead and 30% to the said William Allen and I hereby further appoint the said William Allen to complete and seal and keep going all aeroplane patents of which I may be possessed in the name of my sister Carrie Harker of Maidenhead or in my name and for the use of the aforesaid Benton Aeroplane Works and of the profits of which the said William Allen and my sister Carrie Harker are the sole beneficiaries as stated above and to the aforesaid amounts.

I give and bequeath all the remainder of my property to my sister Carrie Harker of Maidenhead, Berkshire.

Signed:– John Frederick Benton

Signed by the said testator, John Frederick Benton in the presence of us present at the same time, who at his request, in his presence, and in the presence of each other, have subscribed our names as witnesses:–

George Keyte, 31 York Road, Maidenhead
Sabina Rose Allen, 31 York Road, Maidenhead.

This is the Last Will and Testament

- of me -

JOHN FREDERICK PENTON of Lane End High Wycombe in the County of Bucks Gentleman

I HEREBY revoke all former Wills and other testamentary dispositions made by me

I APPOINT as EXECUTORS AND TRUSTEES hereof (hereinafter called "my Trustees") my Solicitor FRANK MEDLICOTT C.B.E., M.P., of 40 Woodville Gardens Ealing in the County of Middlesex and my friend MRS. WINNIE POWLES of 7 Laburnham Road Maidenhead in the County of Berks and I GIVE to the said Mrs. Winnie Powles a legacy of Twenty-five Pounds (£25) (free of Legacy Duty) if she shall act as such Executor

IF I should have survived my friend MRS. SABINA ROSE ALLEN and become entitled to the property known as "Philberds" which stands in our names as joint tenants both at law and in equity then I GIVE DEVISE AND BEQUEATH all my interest in the said property unto my Trustees UPON TRUST to sell the same and out of the proceeds of such sale to pay the sum of One thousand Pounds (£1,000) (free of Legacy Duty) to my niece MISS CAROLINE IRIS VICTORIA HARKER and out of the remainder of the proceeds of the aforesaid sale to pay all legacy duties payable under this my Will and all my debts funeral and testamentary expenses and to divide the balance among the three daughters of my friend Mrs. Sabina Rose Allen namely MRS. ROSE SABINA KEMPTON MRS. DAISY LOUISA TURNER and MRS. IVY EVA TAYLOR in equal shares each for her own use and

12

benefit absolutely

4. I GIVE AND BEQUEATH (free of Legacy Duty) all that part of my estate which consists of investments within the usual meaning of that term (such term however not to include National Savings Certificates or money on deposit or current account at any Bank or in the Post Office Savings Bank) unto my said niece Caroline Iris Victoria Harker

5. I GIVE DEVISE AND BEQUEATH all the rest residue and remainder of my estate both real and personal and whatsoever and wheresoever situate unto my Trustees UPON TRUST for my friend Mrs. Sabina Rose Allen for her own use and benefit absolutely

6. THE said Frank Medlicott and any other Executor or Trustee of this my Will being a Solicitor shall be entitled to charge and to be paid for all professional and other work done by him or by his firm in connection with the trusts of this my Will or the administration of my estate notwithstanding that such work could have been done by a Trustee personally

IN WITNESS whereof I have hereunto set my hand to this my Will this *seventh* day of *December* One thousand nine hundred and forty seven

SIGNED by the said JOHN FREDERICK BENTON as and for his last Will and Testament in the presence of us both being present at the same time who at his request in his presence and in the presence of each other have hereunto subscribed our names as witnesses:-

John Frederick Benton

Schooling

In a letter dated 11th March 1903, old Chris Jorss states that his son John attended a school in the Waterloo district of Sydney.

The following is a list of schools in that area at that time:

Central

Clearbank

Waterloo Estate

The family is known to have lived in the Redfern district of Sydney, this is a list of schools in that area:

Redfern Central

Redfern West

Chippendale

Bullanming Street

Redfern C of E

Redfern R C

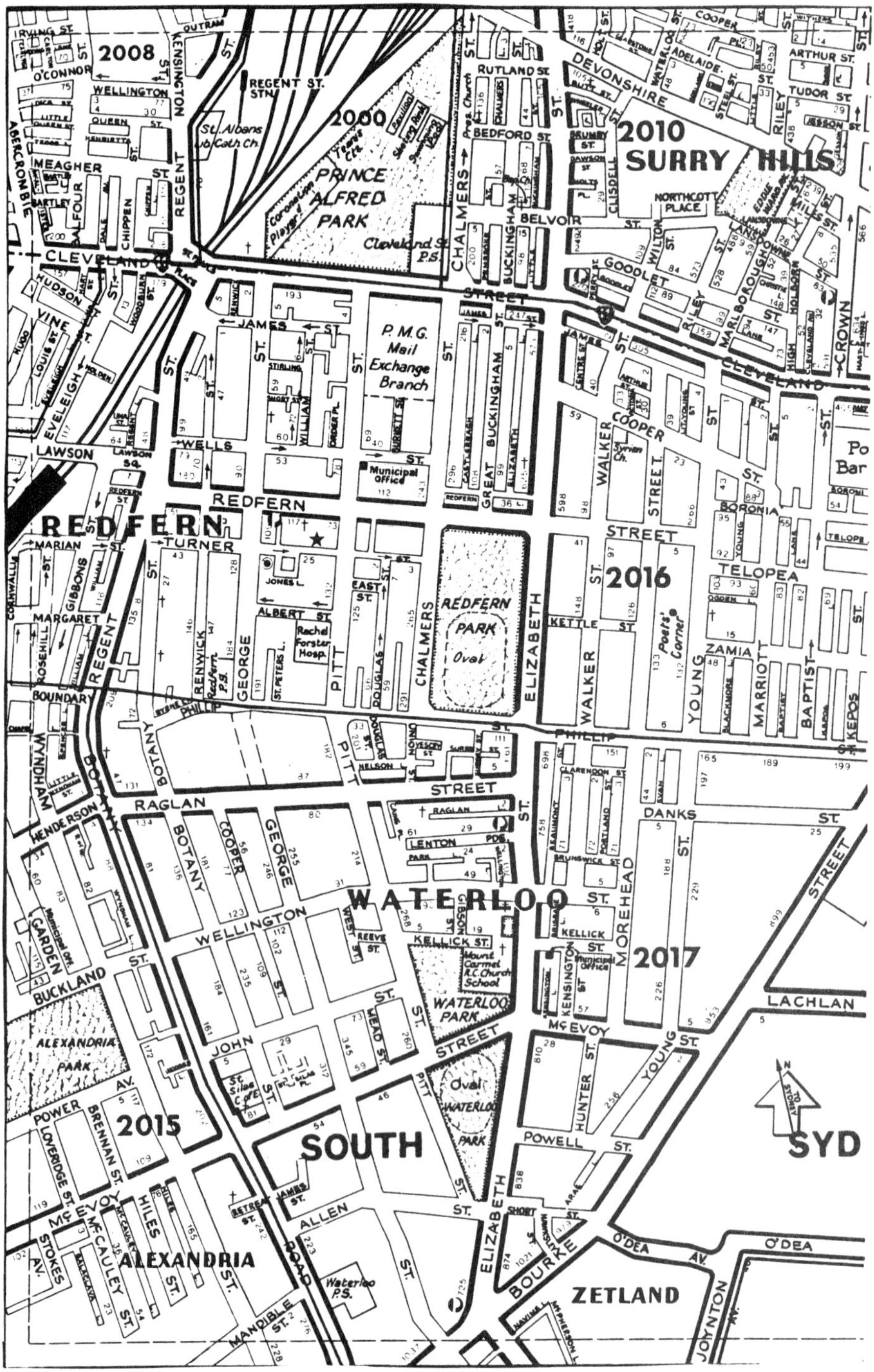
REDFERN
WATERLOO
SOUTH
ALEXANDRIA
ZETLAND
SURRY HILLS
SYD
2008
2000
2010
2016
2017
2015
PRINCE ALFRED PARK
Coronation Playgr'd
Tennis Ct.
Pavilion
Skating Rink
Swimming Pool
Cleveland St. P.S.
St. Albans Lib. Cath. Ch.
REGENT ST. STN
P.M.G. Mail Exchange Branch
Municipal Office
REDFERN PARK Oval
Rachel Forster Hosp.
Redfern P.S.
Poets' Corner
NORTHCOTT PLACE
Syrian Ch.
Mount Carmel R.C. Church School
WATERLOO PARK
Oval WATERLOO PARK
ALEXANDRIA PARK
St. Silas C of E
Waterloo P.S.
Municipal Off.
TO SYDNEY
IRVING ST.
O'CONNOR
WELLINGTON
QUEEN ST.
HENRIETTA
ABERCROMBIE
MEAGHER ST.
BALFOUR
CHIPPEN
KENSINGTON ST.
REGENT ST.
OUTRAM
CLEVELAND
CLEVELAND ST.
HUDSON
VINE
EVELEIGH
LAWSON
LAWSON SQ.
WELLS
JAMES ST.
STIRLING
WILLIAM
REDFERN
TURNER
MARIAN
GIBBONS
MARGARET
CORNWALLIS
ROSEHILL
BOUNDARY
REGENT
RENWICK
GEORGE
ALBERT ST.
JONES L.
ST. PETERS L.
PITT
EAST ST.
DOUGLAS
CHALMERS
ELIZABETH
GREAT BUCKINGHAM
BUCKINGHAM
RUTLAND ST.
BEDFORD ST.
BELVOIR
DEVONSHIRE
COOPER
ADELAIDE
ARTHUR ST.
TUDOR ST.
JESSON ST.
RILEY
CLISDELL
WILTON
GOODLET
LANSDOWNE
MARLBOROUGH
HOLBORN
CROWN
WALKER
COOPER
BORONIA
TELOPEA
STREET
KETTLE ST.
YOUNG
ZAMIA
MARRIOTT
BAPTIST
KEPOS
PHILLIP
WYNDHAM
BOTANY
NELSON
RAGLAN
STREET
DANKS ST.
CLARENDON ST.
BEAUMONT
PORTLAND
BRUNSWICK ST.
LENTON PDE.
MOREHEAD
HENDERSON
GARDEN
BUCKLAND
WELLINGTON
COOPER
GEORGE
KELLICK ST.
KELLICK
KENSINGTON
GIBSON
REEVE
MEAD ST.
JOHN
McEVOY
McEVOY ST.
YOUNG ST.
HUNTER
POWELL ST.
LACHLAN
STREET
POWER
AV.
BRENNAN ST.
LOVERIDGE ST.
HILES ST.
McCAULEY ST.
STOKES AV.
RETREAT
JAMES ST.
ALLEN
ELIZABETH
SHORT
BOURKE
O'DEA AV.
O'DEA
JOYNTON AV.
MANDIBLE ST.
ROAD
McPHERSON L.

Application No. 4958   School No. 505

United Westminster Schools.

Form of Application for Admission to

THE DAY SCHOOL, PALACE STREET, S.W.

When Admission is desired (subject to Vacancy) _at once_
Boy's Name in full _John Burton_
Age last Birthday _12_ Years on _26_ day of _Sept._ 189_5_
Present or recent School _Miss Woods Grenville Sch. Queen's_
Parish in which resident _Westminster St. Margaret's_
Name of Parent or Guardian _Christina Burton_
Occupation _Not any_
Postal Address _137 Victoria St. S.W._

It is understood and agreed that the Fees of the above-named Pupil shall be paid in advance, term by term; and that two months' notice of his removal shall be given, or a half-term's fee paid by me in lieu of notice.

Signed _Christina Burton_

Date _13th April 96_

This Form, when filled up, to be returned to the Clerk (Office at the School), together with One Shilling for Registration Fee. C.r.s

United Westminster (Endowed) Schools.

Middle Class Public Day School
FOR 850 BOYS,
PALACE STREET, VICTORIA STREET, WESTMINSTER.
NEAR VICTORIA STATION.

NEXT TERM BEGINS SEPTEMBER 12th, 1898
(When there will be Vacancies).

Head Master:
Mr. ROBERT F. H. GOFFIN,
Honoursman, Gold Medallist, &c.,
Assisted by a large staff of highly qualified Masters.

Subjects taught:
ENGLISH, FRENCH, GERMAN, LATIN, DRAWING, MATHEMATICS, SCIENCE, VOCAL MUSIC, DRILL, &c.

EXCELLENT BUILDINGS AND LARGE PLAYGROUNDS,
CRICKET FIELD, FIVES COURTS, ATHLETICS, &c.

Separate Rooms for every Class (each under a qualified Master), Laboratories, Lecture Rooms, Drawing School, &c.

WELL-FITTED BOYS' WORKSHOPS.
CARPENTRY—TURNERY—METAL WORKING.

VALUABLE EXHIBITIONS AND SCHOLARSHIPS IN AND FROM THE SCHOOL.

Recent Successes at Examinations held by the undermentioned Public Bodies:—

LONDON UNIVERSITY.
The 10th, 14th, 17th, 35th, 43rd, and 95th, Place in Honours, and Forty in First Class. Eleven Intermediate B.A., two Intermediate B.Sc. Examination, one B.A.

OXFORD AND CAMBRIDGE UNIVERSITY LOCAL.
Over Three hundred have passed, Seventy in Honours, with the *First* and *Fifth* Places in Natural Philosophy for the Kingdom.

CITY AND GUILDS OF LONDON.
Ten Scholarships of £30 a year for two years.

SCHOLARSHIPS AWARDED BY GOVERNORS.
Thirty Scholarships of £30 a year for three years have recently been given.

TWO OPEN SCHOLARSHIPS OF £100 EACH; THREE £52 10s., SIX OF £30 EACH, AND ONE OF £40, WERE OBTAINED BY BOYS OF THIS SCHOOL IN 1889-97.

CIVIL SERVICE OPEN COMPETITION.
At recent Examinations for Boy Clerkships, the *First (thrice), Second, Third, Fifth, Eighth, Ninth, Fifteenth, Nineteenth,* and *Twenty-fifth* places have been taken by Boys at this School. At the two last Examinations Sixty places have been taken.

SOCIETY OF ARTS EXAMINATION IN ARITHMETIC.
Thirty-five passed at recent Examinations.

INCLUSIVE TERMS FOR TUITION AND BOOKS, &c.
Entrance Fee . . . . . 10s.
Upper Division - £2 5s. per Term. | Lower Division £1 12s. 6d. per Term.
There are Three Terms in a year. No extra charges whatever.

Hot Luncheons provided daily, 8d.

Prospectus and Forms of Application free on application to the Clerk or Head Master at the School.

PALACE STREET,   C. SPENCER SMITH,
VICTORIA STREET, S.W.   *Clerk and Receiver.*

A poster which was used to publicise the school in 1898

CITY & GUILDS OF LONDON INSTITUTE FOR THE ADVANCEMENT OF TECHNICAL EDUCATION. *John Watney, Honorary Secretary.*

CENTRAL TECHNICAL COLLEGE,
Exhibition Road.
London, S.W.

September 1900.

Dear Sir,

I have the pleasure to inform you that you have succeeded in passing the Matriculation Examination.

The Course of Study begins on Tuesday, October 2nd, at 10 a.m.

Very truly yours,

Dean.

A. F. Fenton Esq.
4. Wordsworth Mansions,
Queens Club Gardens

United Westminster Schools,
Palace Street, S.W.

Sep. 4 1911

Dear Sir

Benton had better go to the Central Institute & get the form & bring it to me next Monday when I will put in proper letter.

Yours very truly
Robert H. Coffin

Certificate of Birth received 5.9.00
" " " returned 26.9.00 Lr

–201–

City and Guilds of London Institute

Course:- E.E.
Sessions:- 1900/01 & 2 Terms 1901/02 /su JOHN WATNEY, *Honorary Secretary.*   243
Award:- 1st Class Certificate.

CENTRAL TECHNICAL COLLEGE, EXHIBITION ROAD, S.W.

FORM to be filled up by CANDIDATE FOR MATRICULATION, or person wishing to attend a Complete Course of Instruction.

Name (in full) *John Benton Fredrick Benton.*
Age last Birthday† *seventeen* (Date of Birth *Sept. 26/1882*)
Particulars of previous education or employment in practical work *educated at Westminster City School for 4 years was in Upper VI when he left. Attended practical work in work shops and laboratories.*

Particulars as to tenure and value of any Scholarship now held ———
Nil.

Department the Candidate proposes to enter* *Electrical engineering.*
Signature of Parent or Guardian *F.W.Harker.*
Occupation and Address of ditto *4 Wordsworth Mansions Queens Club Gardens. W.*

In the event of my being admitted as a student, I hereby undertake to conform to the Rules of the College as printed on the back of this form.

Signature of Candidate *Jack Benton.*
Address of Candidate *4 Wordsworth Mansions Queens Club Gardens W.*
Date *September 4th/1900.*

* NOTE.—The three Departments of the College are (a) Civil and Mechanical Engineering ; (b) Electrical Engineering ; (c) Chemistry. Students select the department in which they are to be classed, before entering the College. If a student wishes, at the end of the First Year Course, to change his department, application must be made to the Board of Studies before the commencement of a Session. Permission to change can only be given when, in the opinion of the Board, the department selected is not already full.
† A Certificate of Birth and the matriculation fee of £1 should be forwarded with this form to the Honorary Secretary, Central Technical College, Exhibition Road, S.W., a fortnight before the Examination.

ARTER, A. M. (C. & M. 1900–01). M.I.A.E.

Apprentice, Messrs. John I. Thornycroft & Co. Engineer, Messrs. The Long Acre Motor Car Co. Director, Messrs. Marshall Arter & Co. Formed Company—Messrs. Marshall-Arter, Ltd. Works Manager, Messrs. British Ensign Co., Ltd. Consulting Engineer and Adviser to Car Owners.

Paper :—" Indicating High-Speed Steam-Engines," Inst.C.E., 1902.

Special distinction :—Miller Prize, Inst.C.E., 1902, for above paper.

ATKINSON-CLARK, H. G. (E.E. 1900–01).

Land Agent. Managing Director, Normanby Estate Co. Managing Director, Messrs. Crosby Ironstone Co.

Special distinction :—Chairman, Tickhill (Yorks) Urban District Council.

BALFOUR-MURPHY, W. J. (E.E. 1900–02). LL.D. (Heidelberg), F.R.G.S.

With the L.C.C. Tramways. Capt., R. Marines.

Special work :—Conversion of first sections of L.C.C. Tramways from Horse Traction to Electric Conduit system.

Book :—" The Rise and Fall of Nations."

BAXTER, H. H., A.C.G.I. (C. & M. 1900–03).

2nd Lieut., Forfar and Kincardine Artillery, 1903 ; Lieut., 1904 ; Commission R.A., 1905. (No further record.)

BENDER, W. E. G., C.I.E., M.B.E., V.D., A.C.G.I., Siemens Memorial Scholar (C. & M. 1900–03). M.Inst.C.E.

With Messrs. Sir Alexander Rendel & Robertson, London, S.W. Assistant Engineer, Khada Sub-Division, G. Bagaha Extension, B. & I.V.D. Railway. Assistant Engineer, Bengal & N.W. Railway. Capt., I.A.R.O. Resident Engineer, Bengal & N.W. Railway ; Personal Assistant to the General Manager, and Executive Engineer. Chief Engineer, Civil Engineering Department, B. & N.W. and Rohilkund & Kumaon Railways.

Special work :—Responsible for the construction of about 125 miles Metre gauge Railway Extension of the B. & N.W. Railway ; also Locomotive Shops, Gorakhpur ; also for 60 miles Standard Gauge Railway, Samarra to Baiji, during the War (Mesopotamia).

Special distinctions :—M.B.E. (Mil. Div.) (for War Services in Mesopotamia). V.D. (for services in Auxiliary Force, India, Cavalry). Mentioned in Despatches (European War). C.I.E. (New Year Honours, 1936).

BENTON, J. F. (E.E. 1900–02).

With Messrs. The Marconi Wireless Telegraph Co.

BLENKINSOP, P. (Chem. 1900–02).

Director and Chief Chemist, then Managing Director, Messrs. May & Baker, Chemists, London, S.W. Managing Director, Messrs. British Lead Mills, Ltd.

BORNS, G. W. M., M.C., A.C.G.I. (C. & M. 1900–03). A.M.Inst.C.E.

Improver, Messrs. Marshall, Sons & Co., Ltd., Gainsborough. Assistant Engineer, Messrs. Rother Vale Collieries, Ltd., Rotherham. Major, R.E. Manager, Messrs. W. Singleton Birch & Sons, Ltd., Manchester.

Special distinctions :—Military Cross ; mentioned in Despatches (European War).

BOUSFIELD, E. G. P. (E.E. 1900–02).

Manager, Experimental Works, Messrs. Henry Simon, Ltd., Manchester. Managing Director, Messrs. The Saxon Iron & Steel Works, Stoke-on-Trent. Managing Director, Messrs. Metal Finishers, Ltd., London. Relinquished Engineering, and has become a Specialist in Nervous Diseases.

A page from the City and Guilds Register, 1936 (E E:– Electrical Engineering)

THE
MARCONI INTERNATIONAL MARINE COMMUNICATION COMPANY,
LIMITED.

AUTHORISED CAPITAL - - - £350,000.
DIVIDED INTO 350,000 SHARES OF £1 EACH.

Directors.

JOSEPH DE VOLDER (*President*), BRUSSELS.
MAJOR SAMUEL FLOOD PAGE (*Managing Director*), LONDON.
COLONEL ALBERT THYS (*Managing Director for the Continent*), BRUSSELS.
GUGLIELMO MARCONI (*Technical Adviser*), LONDON.
MAURICE TRAVAILLEUR (*Acting Manager for the Continent*), BRUSSELS.
CHARLES BALSER, BRUSSELS.
JAMES FITZGERALD BANNATYNE, LONDON.
HENRY JAMESON DAVIS, LONDON.
COLONEL SIR CHARLES EUAN SMITH, K.C.B., LONDON.
ADOLPH VON HANSEMANN, BERLIN.
ISIDOR LOEWE, BERLIN.
SEGISMUNDO MORET Y PRENDERGAST, MADRID.
GEORGE NAGELMACKERS, PARIS.
ALBERT LIONEL OCHS, LONDON.
LEOPOLD RENOUARD, PARIS.
CHARLES ROUX, MARSEILLES.
HENRY SPEARMAN SAUNDERS, LONDON.
EDGAR ST. PAUL DE SINCAY, PARIS.

Auditors.
MESSRS. COOPER BROTHERS & CO.

Solicitors.
MESSRS. HOLLAMS, SONS, COWARD & HAWKSLEY.

Manager.
H. CUTHBERT HALL.

Marine Superintendent.
CAPTAIN C. V. DALY.

Secretaries and Offices.
HENRY W. ALLEN, 18, FINCH LANE, LONDON, E.C.
GASTON PÉRIER, (for the Continent) 13, RUE BRÉDÉRODE, BRUSSELS.

DIRECTORS' REPORT.

The Directors beg to submit to the Shareholders their First Annual Report and Statement of Accounts from the commencement of the Company to the 30th June, 1901, and they have pleasure in stating that the business of the Company is being firmly established according to the project laid down on its incorporation.

Your Directors have been engaged in England and in many parts of the Continent in using their influence to further the adoption of Marconi Wireless Telegraphy for Maritime purposes by all countries on an International basis, and they are well satisfied with the success so far attained.

Marconi Stations have already been erected on various points of the Coast of Great Britain and Ireland at—

Withernsea,	Holyhead,
Caister,	Port Stewart,
North Foreland,	Rosslare,
The Lizard,	Crookhaven,

and at La Panne, Belgium; Borkum Lighthouse, Borkum Riff Lightship, Germany. In addition to which the following Stations have been equipped by Marconi's Wireless Telegraph Co., Ld., and are available for communication—

Nantucket Lightship,
Siasconset, U.S.A.;

and we are daily expecting to hear that the Station at Belle Isle—entrance to Gulf of St. Lawrence, Canada—is ready for communication.

The greater part of the period now under review was taken up in negotiations, and in laying the foundation of the business, and about two months before the close of the financial year this long period of labour led to satisfactory contracts being made with the shipping companies. Negotiations are going on with several Governments on the Continent and elsewhere.

In England, the Company has entered into an arrangement with "Lloyd's," by which they have definitely adopted the Marconi system and will not use any other system of Wireless Telegraphy at or in connection with their Signal Stations; the Company has undertaken to instal Signal Stations for "Lloyd's," which they will also work for passenger and commercial traffic for the benefit of this Company.

With respect to the Steamship Companies, the Cunard Company, the Norddeutscher Lloyd, La Compagnie Transatlantique, Beaver Line, &c., &c., and the Belgian Mail Packets are already successfully and practically employing the Standard Marconi apparatus on their ships, and this example is likely soon to be followed by all the principal Liners.

Agencies of this Company have been established by our Brussels Office in Paris and Rome, and the negotiations now on foot in the various Continental Countries should lead to the desired expansion and extension of the Company's business.

The following Directors retire by rotation, Messrs. C. BALSER, J. F. G. BANNATYNE, G. NAGELMACKERS, L. RENOUARD, H. S. SAUNDERS, A. VON HANSEMANN, who being eligible, offer themselves for re-election.

Messrs. COOPER BROTHERS & CO., the Auditors, also retire, and offer themselves for re-appointment.

By order of the Board.

HENRY W. ALLEN,
Secretary.

18, FINCH LANE,
LONDON, E.C.,
24th October, 1901.

MARCONI'S WIRELESS TELEGRAPH COMPANY LTD
TELEGRAPHIC ADDRESS.
EXPANSE, LONDON.
TELEPHONE No. 2748, AVENUE.
A.B.C. and WESTERN UNION CODES USED

18, Finch Lane,
London, 14th March '02
E.C.

Mr G. L. Benton,
50 Maury Road,
Stoke Newington.

Dear Sir,

Professor Ayrton has mentioned your name to us in connection with some vacancies which we have for Electrical Students wishing to qualify as Electricians in connection with Wireless Telegraphy. The tuition at our school at Frinton is free. In fact we pay our students 10/- per week and their maintenance from the day they join. If you wish to take up the work, which is extremely interesting, we shall be pleased to see you here any time next week.

Yours faithfully,
Andrew Gray
per pro
MARCONI'S WIRELESS TELEGRAPH Co., Ltd.

An Agreement made the *12th Day of May* 1902 BETWEEN MARCONI'S WIRELESS TELEGRAPH COMPANY LIMITED, of London, (hereinafter referred to as the Company), and *John Frederick Benton, 50, Maury Road, Stoke Newington.*

WHEREBY IT IS MUTUALLY AGREED AS FOLLOWS :—

1. *John Frederick Benton* shall enter into or continue in the service of the Company as the case may be as *Junior Electrician* at the Company's works at Chelmsford or elsewhere and shall perform such duties for the Company and at such place as the Directors or duly appointed officials appointed by them shall from time to time direct and shall obey and conform to all instructions and directions relating to such duties which may be given either by the Directors or by duly authorized persons appointed by them for the time being.

2. *John Frederick Benton,* shall at all times during the said term well and faithfully serve the Company devoting his whole time and attention to its service and using his best endeavours to further and promote its interests. He shall not during his service either on his own account or as the employé of others alone or in conjunction with any other person or persons directly or indirectly be engaged or concerned in any other business or engagement.

3. The Company shall pay to *John Frederick Benton* the sum of *(15/-) Fifteen shillings per week with reasonable travelling and maintenance expense* provided that *John Frederick Benton* is fulfilling his duties to the complete satisfaction of the Directors as to which the decision of the Directors shall be final.

4. *John Frederick Benton,* shall not during the continuance of his engagement or during a further period of three years after the termination of the engagement without the written consent of the Directors first obtained divulge or make known any of the secrets or methods or processes which may at any time during his engagement be or have been employed by the Company in their manufactory or directly or indirectly either on his own account or as the employé of others or alone or in conjunction with any other person or persons engage or be concerned or interested in any similar manufacture or business to that of the Company or any part or branch thereof within 50 miles of London.

5. *John Frederick Benton* shall communicate to the Company every improvement new invention or discovery in connection with or having any relation to any of the articles manufactured or any of the processes or methods employed by the Company which he may make or become possessed of during the engagement which

shall become the property of the Company and *John Frederick Benton* shall if and when required by the Company at the expense of the Company do and execute all acts deeds and things which may be necessary for the purpose of enabling the Company to obtain Letters Patent for the United Kingdom or documents in the nature of Letters Patent for any other country for every such new invention or discovery as aforesaid either in his own name or in conjunction with such other person or persons as the Company may nominate and will if and when required by the Company assign the said Letters Patent or documents to the Company at their expense and will leave it to the discretion of the Directors for the time being whether they shall pay him any compensation and will accept their decision as final.

6. *John Frederick Benton* hereby irrevocably appoints the Secretary of the Company for the time being his Attorney during the continuance of this Agreement for him and in his name and as his act and deed to perform such acts and things and to execute all such deeds and documents as may be necessary for obtaining any such Letters Patent or documents in the nature of Letters Patent referred to in Clause 5 or for assigning the same to the Company *John Frederick Benton*, hereby agreeing to ratify and confirm whatever the said Attorney shall do in or about the premises by virtue of these presents.

7. The engagement may be determined (without prejudice to Clause 4 hereof) at any time upon the Directors giving to *John Frederick Benton* one month's notice in writing of their intention to do so or paying him one month's salary in lieu of notice or on his giving one month's notice in writing to the Secretary of the Company.

8. If any dispute or difference shall arise between the Company and *John Frederick Benton*, as to the construction of this Agreement or any clause thereof or any act or thing to be done hereunder or as to any other matter or thing in any way relating to or arising out of this Agreement the same shall be referred to the arbitration of the Board of Directors of the Company whose decision shall be final and binding upon both sides to the exclusion of any other mode of reference or arbitration.

In Witness whereof the said
John Frederick Benton
hath hereunto set his hand this
12th day of May 1902.

John Frederick Benton

Witness:—
Y. W. Harker
5C. Maury Road
Stoke Newington

MARCONI'S WIRELESS TELEGRAPH COMPANY LTD
TELEGRAPHIC ADDRESS.
EXPANSE, LONDON.
TELEPHONE N° 2748, AVENUE.
A.B.C. AND WESTERN UNION CODES USED

18, Finch Lane,
London, 19th Nov 1902
E.C.

A.P

Mr. J.E.Benton.

Dear Sir,

    The Directors have had under their consideration the question of maintenance of the technical staff and consider it advisable to adopt new arrangements, full particulars of which are given in the enclosed circular.

    Under the new arrangements you will be required to provide your own maintenance from the 1st January next and in consideration of this you will receive an increase of salary of £1 per week.

    I have pleasure in also informing you that the Directors have decided to increase your salary to £46.0.0 per annum from the 1st November, so that under the new arrangement your salary from the 1st January next will be £100.0.0 per annum.

    Kindly acknowledge receipt of this letter and signify your acceptance of the change.

                  Yours faithfully,
              MARCONI'S WIRELESS TELEGRAPH Co. Ltd.

                    Henry Allen
                    SECRETARY & ASST MANAGER

Enclo;

Hotel and travelling expenses of the Technical staff

The following arrangements will come into force on the 1st January 1903.

FARES: In Great Britain, third class Railway and second class Boat Fares, in Ireland and on the Continent, second class Railway and Boat Fares and on Transatlantic Boats first class fares will be allowed. In Ireland, in the event of second class Railway accommodation not being available, first class will be allowed. When travelling through the night, second class Railway Fare allowed in all cases. If second class accommodation is not available, first class will be allowed.

TRAVELLING EXPENSES: When meals are necessary on Railway journeys, or Assistants are staying for a few hours at any place where they will not spend the night, an allowance will be made of 1/3, 2/- and 3/- for Breakfast, Lunch and Dinner respectively.

MAINTENANCE: On and after the 1st January 1903, the Technical Staff will provide their own maintenance; excepting under the following conditions:–

1. When moving from one place to another in the United Kingdom and on the Continent an allowance will be made of 8/6 for each of the first seven nights after arrival at destination to include day expenses between one night and another in the same place and to cover extra expense incurred owing to change of residence.

2. When members of the staff are sent to Stations where special hotel arrangements have been made for the maintenance of the Company's Staff the preceding paragraph will not apply and Assistants will instead reside at the Hotel for seven nights at the expense of the Company.

At present the Hotels for which arrangements have been made are Poldhu and Haven.

HOLIDAYS: Fourteen days will be allowed annually.

Tyneside.—In a short time the tramways between Wallsend and North Shields are expected to be completed, and it will then be possible to journey from Newcastle almost to Whitley Bay by tram. There will be only one break, that between Walker and Wallsend.

Withington.—The B. of T. has prolonged the period allowed for the completion of the U.D.C.'s electric tramway for a year.

TELEGRAPH AND TELEPHONE NOTES.

Brighton Telephones.—The Telephones Committee of the T.C. has recommended that the installation of the municipal telephone system should be proceeded with as soon as possible, and that Mr. Bennett, engineer, should prepare estimates of the cost of the scheme. Exclusive of the Corporation connections, 831 persons have promised to become subscribers, and already £3,710 has been expended in laying underground ducts, &c.

The German Atlantic Cables.—We learn from th Deutsch-Atlantische Telegraphengesellschaft that the cable ship *Vo Podbielski* returned on July 23rd from a sounding expedition on the line of the company's proposed second cable, and that the trace o the latter has been definitely decided upon. The manufactur of the first section has also been taken in hand, and is makin satisfactory progress.

International Telephones.—On August 15th th international telephone lines between Como, Chiasso, Genoa, Turi and France were opened to the public. Between Genoa and Turi the fee for service is one lira (10d.). Between Genoa and Franc the rates are 3, 3·50 and 4·50 lire according to the distance. Th work of the Rome, Turin, Milan line had to be stopped owing tc the lack of bronze wire, which is being manufactured at Berge (Norway).

The Shah's Visit.—The Shah of Persia granted ar audience on Tuesday at Marlborough House, to a deputation from the Board of Directors of the Indo-European Telegraph Company consisting of Messrs. J. Herbert Tritton, Chas. Holland, and T. W Stratford-Andrews, chairman and directors of the company. The directors presented an address on behalf of the company, giving expression of their grateful acknowledgment for the protection to the company's line (which traverses Persian territory and terminates in Teheran, the capital of that country) enjoyed so long under the beneficent rule of the Imperial Persian Government. The address, embellished on the model of ancient Persian art, was contained in a silver-gilt casket of beautiful workmanship in Oriental style, and emblematical of telegraphs and the commerce of the British Empire and Persia, surmounted by a finely modelled figure of Mercury, holding in one hand the caduceus of commerce, and with the other gathering electric fluid. The address was graciously received by his Majesty.

Telegraphic Interruptions and Repairs :—

CABLES.	INTERRUPTED.	REPAIR
Latakia-Cyprus	..	June 30, 1899 ..
Communication with Carthagena and Barran- quilla (Colombia)	..	Dec. 8, 1900
Trinidad-Demerara No. 1	..	Aug. 27, 1901
Communication with Bolama	..	April 18, 1902
St. Lucia-St. Vincent	..	May 8, 1902
St. Lucia-Grenada	..	May 8, 1902
Dominica-Martinique	..	May 8, 19
St. Lucia-Martinique	..	May 8.
Guadeloupe-Martinique	..	May
Santa Cruz de Teneriffe to Tejita de Teneriffe	Jul	
Puerto Plata-Martinique	J	,902
Guantanamo-Mole St. Nicholas	..	, 1902
Nagasaki-Fusan (between Tsushima and Fusa	o, 1902	
Cape Town-St. Helena	..	¢. 15, 1902 .. August 10
Cape Town-Mossamedes	..	.ug. 15, 1902 ..
Cayenne-Pinheiro	..	Aug. 18, 1902 ..

LANDLINES :—

Route via Hanekin on Persian		Feb. 24, 1900	..
Communication with Tientsin Helampo	akn via	July 18, 1900	..
Communication with Juneau,	a	Aug. 18, 1902	..

West Hartlepool Telephones.—The T.C. has decided to apply to the Postmaster-General for a telephone license for the Hartlepools area.

Wireless Telegraphy.—The *Chronicle* Brussels correspondent says that the Congo Free State is at present making important experiments in wireless telegraphy, the results of which will show what may be expected from wireless "wires" as applied to communication on land. Lieutenant de Bremaeker, of the Belgian "Engineers," has just completed a Marconi installation at Banana, in the Congo, composed of a telegraph pole over 70 yards high, provided at the base with a portable cabin for the instruments. A petroleum motor drives a dynamo used for charging the accumulators that supply the necessary electric current to the induction coils. Working in connection with this station will be another on Portuguese territory 75 miles distant, and at present being installed by Lieutenant de Bremaeker at Ambrizette. It is considered that the immense mountain separating these two stations contributes a fair sample of the maximum transmission obstruction to be met with in wireless installations, even in hilly countries. The experiment is costing the Congo Free State administration 25,000 fr.

It is stated that the French Government has decided to instal the Marconi system in all the ports of Algeria and Tunisia.

The *London Gazette* states that information, dated July 7th, 1902, has been received from the Marconi Wireless Telegraph Company, Limited, that stations have been established by it at the undermentioned places, and that messages can be received at these stations and forwarded to their destinations :—1. Frinton-on-Sea, Essex. 2. North Foreland, Kingsgate. 3. Niton, near St. Catherine's Point, Isle of Wight. 4. Haven, northern entrance to Poole Harbour. 5. Lizard, a quarter of a mile westward of Lloyd's signal station. 6. Holyhead, in the town. 7. Rosslare, three-quarters of a mile north of railway station. 8. Crookhaven, half-a-mile westward of village. 9. Malin Head, Lloyd's signal station. 10. Innistrahull, Lloyd's signal station. 11. Borkum, River Ems, Germany. 12. Borkum Light Vessel, Germany. 13. Nieuport, Belgium. 14. Belle Isle, Labrador. 15. Chateau Bay, Labrador. 16. Sagaponack, near Sag Harbour, Long Island, U S A.

THE MARCONI INTERNATIONAL MARINE COMMUNICATION COMPANY, LTD.

TELEGRAPHIC ADDRESS,
EXPANSE, LONDON.
TELEPHONE Nº 2748 AVENUE.
A.B.C. AND WESTERN UNION CODES USED.
Continental Office,
48, RUE DE NAMUR,
BRUSSELS.

18, Finch Lane,
London, E.C.

20th February 1903.

Mr J. F. Benton,
    Assistant Electrician,
        9, Hall Street, CHELMSFORD.

Dear Sir,

The Directors propose to engage you on foreign service to occupy the position of Assistant Electrician on the work in connection with carrying out the contract between the Company and the Congo Free State for establishing wireless telegraphic communication between Banana and Ambrizette, or between other places in the Congo Free State, or Portuguese West Africa, on the following conditions:-

The engagement to commence from February 24th 1903 for three months certain, and to be prolonged at the Company's option for any further period not exceeding twelve months from the commencement of the Agreement.

Your salary will be at the rate of £120 per annum and during the continuance of the Agreement, the Company will bear all your travelling and maintenance expenses.

You will take your instructions from the Engineer in charge of the work, or other duly authorised officer of the

THE MARCONI INTERNATIONAL MARINE COMMUNICATION CO., LTD., LONDON.

Mr. J. F. Benton. *Continued.*   Page 2

Company, and you will carry out such instructions to the best of your ability.

On the expiration or earlier termination of the Agreement as after mentioned, the Company will provide you with a first class passage to London and pay to date of arrival.

Notwithstanding anything contained herein this Agreement shall cease and determine by the completion or cancelling of the Company's contract with the Congo Free State from any cause whatsoever, or by sickness rendering your return to England absolutely necessary, but in the former case it will be in the option of the Company to continue your services in the aforesaid capacity on similar work in the above mentioned countries for the full period of the Agreement.

If at the termination of this Agreement, your conduct has been satisfactory to the Directors, you will be granted one month's leave on full foreign service pay for every six months served abroad.

THE MARCONI INTERNATIONAL MARINE Co.
Yours faithfully, LIMITED.

I have read the foregoing and agree to engage for foreign service in the countries and on the terms mentioned herein.

John Frederick Benton.

Witness: Andrew Gray

Serie de 1903   Ill.mo Exm.o Snr.

N.º

   Felicitando V. Ex.ª, pelos
resultados que obteve, rogo a V. Ex.ª
se digne informar-me de quando
terão logar as experiencias of-
ficiaes, afim de eu poder informar
o Governo.
  Desejo vivamente o bom exito dos
seus trabalhos.
       Deus Guarde a V. Ex.ª

Sabrizette 6
de Maio de 903

Ill.mo Exm.o Snr
Chefe da estação
de telegraphia sem
fios

        D'esta
       O Presidente,

Manuel Pedro Ferreira

A translation of document on preceding page.

Series of 1903　　　　　　　　　　Most Illustrious and Excellent Senhor
No 174
I congratulate your Excellency on the results that you have obtained, and beg you to be so kind as to inform me when the official tests will take place, so that I may inform the Government about them.
I heartily wish for good results from your work.
God preserve your Excellency

　　　　　　　　　　　　　Ambrizette, 6th May 1903
　　　　　　　　　　　　　The most Illustrious and Excellent Senhor,
　　　　　　　　　　　　　the Chief of the Wireless Station
　　　　　　　　　　　　　"Vesta"
　　　　　　　　　　　　　The Resident
　　　　　　　　　　　　　Manuel Pedro Ferreira,
　　　　　　　　　　　　　(Sant) Antonio do Zaire

ÉTAT INDÉPENDANT DU CONGO.

DÉPARTEMENT DES AFFAIRES ÉTRANGÈRES.

PASSE-PORT.

N° 20

Droit perçu :
Dix francs

SIGNALEMENT :

Âge de 21 ans.
Cheveux *châtains*
Sourcils *"*
Yeux *bruns*
Front *ordinaire*
Nez *"*
Bouche *"*
Menton *"*
Visage *ovale*
Barbe *absente*
Taille 1 m. 60
Signes particuliers : *aucun*

Valable pour *un an*.

(4)

J. Frederick Benton.

AU NOM DU ROI DES BELGES,
SOUVERAIN DE L'ÉTAT INDÉPENDANT DU CONGO,

Nous (1) *Thonne Elie*, *f.f. de Commissaire de District à Banana*

Prions tous les magistrats et officiers, tant civils que militaires, quels qu'ils puissent être, des Princes et Etats étrangers, de laisser passer librement M (2) *Benton John Frederick assistant électricien*

avec ses hardes et bagages, allant à *Emberzelle* sans permettre qu'il lui soit opposé aucune entrave ou empêchement et de lui donner ou faire donner toute aide ou secours, ainsi que nous le ferions nous-même, en étant requis.

Donné à *Banana*, le (3) *quatre avril mil neuf cent et trois*

[signature]

N° 55

ÉTAT INDÉPENDANT DU CONGO

Reçu de *Berton, John Frederic*

Chef de Kinery T.S.F.

la somme de *dix francs*

pour *délivrance d'un passeport*

Banana, le 22 Juin 1904

L'officier de l'état civil

ÉTAT INDÉPENDANT DU CONGO.

DÉPARTEMENT DES AFFAIRES ÉTRANGÈRES.

PASSE-PORT.

N° 50

Droit perçu :
dix francs.

SIGNALEMENT :

Âge de 21 ans.
Cheveux châtain clair
Sourcils
Yeux bruns
Front ordinaire
Nez
Bouche
Menton
Visage ovale
Barbe
Taille 1m.60
Signes particuliers :
Valable pour un an.

(4) J. Frederick Benton

AU NOM DU ROI DES BELGES,
SOUVERAIN DE L'ÉTAT INDÉPENDANT DU CONGO,

Nous (1) Carré Louis Commissaire de District de Banana

Prions tous les magistrats et officiers, tant civils que militaires, quels qu'ils puissent être, des Princes et Etats étrangers, de laisser passer librement M (2) Benton, John Frederic, chef de la mission de la C.S.F.

avec ses hardes et bagages, allant à Ambrizette sans permettre qu'il lui soit opposé aucune entrave ou empêchement et de lui donner ou faire donner toute aide ou secours, ainsi que nous le ferions nous-même, en étant requis.

Donné à Banana, le (3) vingt deux juin mil neuf cent et quatre

Le Commissaire d. Dt d. Banana

Carré

Monsieur Benton est accompagné de trois travailleurs.

(1) Nom, prénoms et qualité du fonctionnaire
(2) Prénoms, nom, qualité, domicile.
(3) Date en toutes lettres.
(4) Signature du porteur.

Visto bom e
que vae a S. Antonio
do Zaire a bordo do
Vapor Bréguedta acompa-
nhado... tres permanentes de acom-
panhamento... Pierre... Pist.
Ambriz, 28 de Junho de 1900
O Residente inte.
Francisco de Rezende

Visto e bom para seguir para
Banana.
Residencia de Santo Antonio do
Zaire, 3 de Julho de 1904.
O Residente

A translation of passport number 50.

INDEPENDENT STATE of the CONGO
Department of Foreign Affairs. Passport.
In the name of the King of Belgium, Sovereign of the Independent State of the Congo.
We (1) Carre Louis, Commissioner of the District Banana:– request all magistrates and officers, whether civilians or military, of the Principality or the Department of Foreign Affairs to let pass without hindrance and freely Mr (2) BENTON, John Frederick, Chief of the Mission of T.I.F. with his clothes and baggages going to Ambrizette, without any opposition or hindrance and to give him every help and succour as we do ourselves when required.
Given at Banana the 22nd June 1904
The Commissioner of the District Banana
Signed: Marie.
Mr Benton is accompanied by three workmen.

Fee received:	10 Francs
Age:	21 years
Hair:	Chestnut Brown
Eyebrows:	do do
Eyes:	Brown
Front:	Normal
Nose:	Normal
Mouth:	Normal
Chin:	Normal
Face:	Oval
Beard:	None
Height:	1.60 metres
Special Features:	
Valid for One Year	
Signed:	Frederick Benton

Translation of notes on the back of passport number 50.
Approved to proceed to Sant' Antoni do Zaire, on board the steamer "Benguela", with three servants named Domingo, Thome and Pedro accompanying him.
Ambrizette, 28th June 1904
The Deputy Resident
Francisco de Resem
Approved to proceed to Banana.
Residency of Sant' Antonio do Zaire, 1st July 1904.
The Resident
(Signature)

Serie de 1904

PROVINCIA DE ANGOLA

SECRETARIA GERAL DO GOVERNO

REPARTIÇÃO POLITICA E CIVIL

2.ª Secção — 1.ª Sub-secção

N.º 56

Ill.mo Ex.mo Sr.

Em referencia ao officio de V. Ex.ª N.º 104-B de 9 de Abril ultimo, encarrega-me Sua Ex.ª o Conselheiro Governador Geral, de participar a V. Ex.ª que resolveu mandar seguir para o Bararra e Ambrizette o director dos telegraphos desta provincia, Francisco Pereira Batalha, afim de assistir ás experiencias a que o mesmo officio se refere, e apresentar-(a Sua Ex.ª) um relatorio dellas, que será enviado ao Governo de Sua Magestade.

Deus Guarde a V. Ex.ª

Secretaria Geral do Governo em Loanda, 16 de Maio de 1904.

Ill.mo Ex.mo Sr. Engenheiro Chefe da Missão de estudos do Telegrapho sem fios.

O Secretario Geral

Translation of letter on preceding page
Series of 1904
Province of Angola.
General Secretariat of the Government.
Political and Civil Department.
Section 3, Subsection 1.
No: 663
Most Illustrious and Excellent Senhor
With reference to your Excellency's letter No. 104.B of 9th April last, his Excellency the Counsellor Governor General instructs me to inform Your Excellency that he has decided to order the Director of Telegraphs for that province, Francisco Pereira Batalha, to proceed to Banana and Ambrizette so as to assist in the tests to which the same letter refers, and to present an account of them to His Excellency, which will be sent to His Majesty's Government.
God preserve your Excellency
The General Secretariat of the Government in Luanda, 16th May 1904.
The most Illustrious and excellent Senhor, the Chief Engineer of the Research Mission for Wireless Telegraphy.
The Secretary General
(Signature)

PROVINCIA DE ANGOLA
Governo do districto do Congo

Passaporte do Interior

SIGNAES
- Idade: 26 annos
- Altura: 1m62
- Rosto: comprido
- Cabellos: cor
- Sobr'olhos: id.
- Olhos: castanhos
- Nariz: regular
- Bocca: regular
- Côr: branca

SIGNAES PARTICULARES

N.º _____
Registado a fl. _____ do liv. _____ de similhantes
Custo do passaporte: $540
Sello: _____

O **Governador** do districto do Congo *José do Nascimento Pinheiro*

Concede passaporte a *J. F. Benton*

natural de *Australia*

para *Ambrizette*, por tempo de *tres* mezes, levando *em sua companhia um creado maior de nome Pessoa*.

Abonado *competentemente*

E cumprindo a obrigação de se apresentar ás auctoridades dos districtos por onde transitar e pernoitar, para lhe visarem o passaporte; manda a todas as auctoridades a quem pertencer o conhecimento d'este, não ponham embaraço ao portador.

Secretaria da residencia de _____

em 15 de Março de 1904.

Por auctorização de S. Ex.ª o Governador do districto,
Pelo residente, _____

Certo bem —
Segue p.ª S. Antonio
do Zaire a bordo do
Vapor Bosquedo
Angola 30 [...] 1904
O Presidente,
[assinatura]

Visto e bom para seguir
para Noqui.
Residencia de [...] Anto
nio do Zaire 1.º de Abril de
1904.
O Residente
[assinatura]

Translation of Angolan passport
PROVINCE OF ANGOLA
GOVERNMENT OF THE DISTRICT OF ANGOLA
PASSPORT FOR THE INTERIOR
THE GOVERNOR of the district of the Congo, Jose do Nascimuito Guilleiro, grants to J F Benton, a citizen of Australia, for Ambrizette, for a period of three months, taking in his company a male servant of full age named Secca.
Properly vouched for.
And provided he complies with the obligation to present himself to the Authorities of the districts, through which he is to pass and in which he is to spend the night, for which they stamp the passport, the Governor commands all the Authorities who are to be aware of, not to cause any impediment to the bearer.
Secretariat of the Residency of Sant' Antonio de Zaire, 15th March 1904.
By authority of his Excellency the Governor of the district,
For the Associate Resident.
Cardosa de Santiago.
Description

Age:	26 years
Height:	1m 62
Face:	Long
Hair:	Fair
Eyebrows:	Same
Eyes:	Brown
Nose:	Regular
Mouth:	Same
Colour:	White

Particular marks:
No:
Registered on Page of the book of such matters.
Charge for Passport:) $540
Seal:)

Translation of notes on back of Angolan passport.
Approved to proceed to Sant' Antonio de Zaire, on board the steamer "Benguela".
Ambrizette, 30th March 1904
The Resident
(Signature)
Approved to proceed to Noqui.
Residency of Sant' Antonio do Zaire, 1st April 1904
The Resident
(Signature)

Compagnie de Télégraphie sans Fil

SOCIÉTÉ ANONYME

Adresse télégraphique
WIRELESS-BRUXELLES
CODE A.B.C. (1883)

B. N° 2334
Annexe
N.B. Prière de rappeler le numéro ci-dessus dans la réponse.

Bruxelles, le 20 Avril 1904.
48, rue de Namur.

Monsieur B e n t o n
Ingénieur
B a n a n a (Congo)

Monsieur,

Nous avons reçu le télégramme de Monsieur De Bremaecker disant: "Benton accept the proposal if wait my letter of this date".

La lettre annoncée ne devant nous parvenir que le 3 mai, nous ne pouvons actuellement nous prononcer sur ce que vous pouvez nous y demander, et nous vous écrirons à ce sujet par le prochain courrier.

Quoiqu'il en soit Monsieur De Bremaecker nous ayant fait savoir qu'il rentrerait par le bateau du 24 Mai, nous vous chargeons de le remplacer à partir d'alors et jusqu'à nouvel avis, comme Chef de notre Mission en Afrique.

Monsieur De Bremaecker vous remettra tous les documents et tous les renseignements nécessaires à cette fin.

La démonstration devant être terminée au 15 Mai, voici les travaux dont nous vous chargeons:

1°.- Démontage du poste d'Ambrizette, emballage de son matériel et transport de celui-ci à Banana.

2°.- Mise en ordre du poste de Banana et remisage du matériel d'Ambrizette à Banana.

3°.- Expédition à Chelmsford du matériel repris pages 3 et 4 de nos Instructions A.A. 205.

4°.- Remise du poste de Banana et du matériel laissé en

COMPAGNIE DE TÉLÉGRAPHIE SANS FIL N° 2. a: Mr. Benton
(Société anonyme)

Afrique à la garde d'un opérateur.

5°.- Visite des terrains à Boma, Banana et St Thomé et retour en Europe comme il est dit dans nos Instructions A.A. 205.

Pour l'exécution de ces divers travaux vous suivrez nos Instructions A.A. 197 pages 3 et 4 et A.A. 205 que vous remettra Monsieur De Bremaecker ainsi que les Instructions complémentaires ci-jointes.

Ci-joint vous trouverez également des Instructions pour l'emploi des fonds et la Comptabilité.

Veuillez noter que nous désirons éviter autant que possible l'envoi de nouveaux agents pour l'achèvement de ces divers travaux. Nous espérons donc que Messieurs Poupart et Winther accepteront en tous cas de rester tous deux en Afrique jusqu'à la fin de ces travaux. Nous espérons même que l'un des deux acceptera de rester en Afrique pour prendre la garde du poste de Banana.

En tous cas veuillez noter que Monsieur Poupart ne peut exiger son rapatriement que par le bateau du 5 Juillet et Monsieur Winther par le bateau du 14 Juin.

Veuillez noter également que si nous devons envoyer un nouvel agent au Congo celui-ci ne pourra quitter Anvers qu'au départ du 2 Juin.

Nous vous donnons ces divers renseignements pour que vous puissiez arranger votre service et celui de vos adjoints de façon à ne pas laisser vos stations sans gardiens.

Il est entendu que vous vous efforcerez de réaliser les divers travaux ci-dessus au mieux des intérêts de la Compagnie et

COMPAGNIE DE TÉLÉGRAPHIE SANS FIL N° 3. à : Mr. Benton
(Société anonyme)

pour tout ce qui n'est pas prévu dans les instructions vous adopterez la solution la plus raisonnable, sauf à justifier vis-à-vis de notre Compagnie à Bruxelles les mesures que vous avez prises.

Il est entendu également que, chaque fois qu'il sera possible, vous ne prendrez aucune mesure importante sans en référer à Bruxelles

Veuillez agréer, Monsieur, l'assurance de notre considération distinguée.

COMPAGNIE DE TÉLÉGRAPHIE SANS FIL
(SOCIÉTÉ ANONYME)

LE SECRÉTAIRE *LE DIRECTEUR*

Translation of three page letter on preceding pages.
Mr Benton, Engineer, Banana, (Congo).
Sir,
We have received Mr De Bremaecker's telegram reading: "Benton accept the proposal if wait my letter of this date".
This letter did not arrive until the 3rd of May, thus we could not actually reply to what you asked us and we are writing you by return of post.
Since Mr De Bremaecker has let us know that he will leave by boat on the 24th May, we instruct you to replace him from that date and until further notice as Chief of our Mission in Africa.
To this end Mr De Bremaecker will hand over to you all the documents and all the necessary information.
The demonstration must finish by the 15th May and herewith the tasks which we require you to execute:–
1. Close down the post at Ambrizette, pack up all its material and transport this to Banana.
2. Put the post at Banana in good order and store the material from Ambrizette at Banana.
3. Send to Chelmsford those materials mentioned on pages 3 and 4 of our instruction A. A 205.
4. Leave the post at Banana and the remaining goods in charge of a caretaker.
5. Visit the areas at Boma, Banana and St Thome and return to Europe as per our instructions A.A 205.

To execute these various tasks follow our instructions A.A 197 pages 3 and 4 and A.A 205 which Mr De Bremaecker will give you as well as the instructions attached herewith.
Also attached you will find the instructions on how to deal with the monies and accounts.
Please note that we would like to avoid, if at all possible, to employ new agents in order to achieve all these tasks.
We hope that Mr Poupart and Mr Winther will accept and in any case that both will agree to stay in Africa until these tasks have been completed. We even hope that one of them will agree to stay in Africa to caretake the post at Banana.
In any case please note that Mr Poupart will not be able to repatriate until he can leave by boat on 5th July and Mr Winther by the boat of 14th June.
Please also note that if we have to appoint a new agent for the Congo he will not be able to leave Antwerp until the 2nd of June.
We inform you of all the above so that you may execute your various tasks and those of your helpers without leaving your stations unmanned.
It is understood that you will do your utmost to carry out your various tasks as undermentioned to the best interest of our Company and in the case of anything arising that we have not anticipated you will follow the best course possible in the interests of our Company in Brussels.
  Also it must be understood that you will not undertake anything important without first referring the matter to Brussels.

WEST AFRICA

Latest Mining Results.

Ashanti Goldfields Corporation.—Crushings for February:—Obuassi Mine, 1,700 tons for 2,400 oz.; development, 1,720 tons for 850 oz. Temporary pumps were installed at Obuassi on February 13 to re-pump tailings water, pending completion of heavy Tompera pumping plant.

Ashanti Sansu.—Crushing for February:—2,000 tons; 590 oz. The new resident manager and his staff arrived at the mine on February 16. As soon as the crosscut from the new shaft reaches the Main Reef the manager will be able to resume former shipments of bullion.

Liberia's New President.

Particulars have just been received from Liberia of the inauguration of the new President, Mr. Arthur Barclay. He is the twenty-eighth President of the Republic, and was born in Bridgetown, Barbados, and was consequently a British subject. He was taken to Liberia when eleven years of age. Shortly before his election to the Presidency he was Secretary of State and then Secretary of the Treasury. The following have been selected as his new Cabinet:—Mr. H. W. Travis, Secretary of State, Mr. D. E. Howard, Secretary of the Treasury; Mr. H. T. Moore, Secretary of the Interior; Mr. R. T. Sherman, Secretary of War; Mr. S. T. Prout, Postmaster-General; Mr. F. E. R. Johnson, Attorney-General.

Sekondi up to Date.

An esteemed correspondent (W. K.), writing from Sekondi on February 18, says:—

With the exception of a few new bungalows and stores, Sekondi is much the same as when I passed through it some months ago. I was fortunate in getting over the railway journey without any delay or mishap, but there is still very much room for improvement. From Sekondi to Obuassi is about 124 miles, and this one is now able to do in one day—a poor record compared with the Scotch express or even the old Z.A.S.M.! The rates are very exorbitant, and in many instances it would be possible to convey light packages by native carriers from the Coast about as cheap as by rail. The mining companies are still very much handicapped by the high rates, but they have the advantage of getting heavy packages delivered in a much shorter time.

School of Tropical Medicine.

The fifth annual report of the Liverpool School of Tropical Medicine states that testimony is constantly arriving from West Africa and other unhealthy regions in the Tropics to the effect that where the recommendations of the school have been followed the health conditions have been much improved. Since the foundation of the school twelve expeditions have been despatched to the Tropics for the study of malaria, yellow fever, trypanosomiasis and sanitation. During the past year 143 cases have been admitted into the tropical ward attached to the school. A new laboratory has been built and equipped with the necessary apparatus. The attendance of students has been very satisfactory, and, as formerly, they have generally been medical officers holding appointments of responsibility. The report appends a list of subscribers to the Sir Alfred Jones Chair of Tropical Medicine (now occupied by Major Ronald Ross, F.R.S.) and to the general funds of the school.

Railway Rates in West Africa.

At the annual general meeting of the Wassaw West Amalgamated Mines, Ltd., held on Monday, the Chairman said:

We have forty miles of railway only from the port, Sekondi, to our property, whereas in South Africa everything has to be carried over between 500 and 600 miles. I need hardly point out that, as regards machinery and plant generally, there is no reason why it should be more expensive for West Africa than it is for South Africa; in fact, the sea route is about half the distance. Although, at the present time, the railway rates are absolutely impossible and extortionate—namely, 2s. 6d. per ton per mile for machinery—it cannot be to the interest of the Government to keep the rates at a level which will prevent the mining industry being carried on profitably in West Africa; and we confidently look forward, in the near future, to an alteration in the rates to something like the prices charged in South and East Africa. I may mention that if you take, for instance, the Uganda Railway, made through a country which pays nothing at all, the Government are willing to meet the East African Syndicate in the most favourable way possible; indeed, they are talking of reducing the rates on certain articles to as low as ½d. per ton per mile from the centre of Africa to the coast. I have no doubt that the Colonial Office will see the necessity for reducing the railway rates in West Africa also.

BRITISH CENTRAL AFRICA

(From "The B.C.A. Times," Blantyre, January 30.)

Good rains continue to fall all over the Shire Highlands. The rainfall, as taken in Blantyre township for the week ending January 30, is 2.77 inches, and for the month to date, 7.06 inches.

Mr. Evans, of the B.C.A. Company, Ltd., returned from furlough this week. After putting into commission the 'Lady of the Lake" and "John Bowie" he will erect at Mpimbi the new cotton machinery coming out for the company for their Upper Shire estates.

Mr. B. Van Hees has been appointed acting manager for the Flotilla Co., which firm, we understand, are now to have their head office in Chinde, where Mr. Van Hees is likely to be resident. Mr. R. B. McAuslan, the popular agent of the company in Blantyre, is at present in charge of the Chiromo and up-country stations.

As a result of the recent heavy rains in Mlanje district, a large number of cotton plants have been washed away.

We regret to hear that Mr. Pratt-Barlow has been invalided, and leaves to-morrow by the B.C.A. Co. Messrs. Vallentine (Z.I.M.), Chettle, and the Oceana prospectors are also travelling by the same company's steamer.

The Oceana Co.'s prospectors, who have finished operations in the Protectorate, left to-day for South Africa. Nothing has transpired as to the result of their work.

The coffee market is showing some signs of recovery. The Z.I.M. got as high as 85s. per cwt. for one lot of five bags, the next best price being 67s. 6d. for five other bags of the same firm's mark. The average prices still run between 40s. and 50s., but this is a slight improvement, and is likely to continue. Chillies continue to find a good market, 58s. per cwt. being obtained by a parcel with the B.E.A.L. mark.

We regret to hear that Mr. Vrebos, who passed through Blantyre recently on his way homeward, but who was taken ill at Katungas with blackwater fever, has succumbed to his illness. Mr. Cooper, the A.L.C. agent, very kindly attended him during the week he was ill.

The new electric power station at Zomba is now rapidly approaching completion, and is in every way a substantial structure. Not only have present needs been seen to, but also those well into the future, the result being that work will be carried on with a minimum expenditure. The new dynamos are expected to arrive from Chinde shortly.

The African Lakes Corporation steamers *Duchess*, *Henry Henderson*, and *Scott*, have all been up at Katungas this week with cargo, but the river is now falling considerably again, and unless further rains fall locally navigation to Katungas will again be at a standstill, as there is not nearly sufficient water from the Lake to keep things going.

A serious wash-away on the Katunga road has occurred, which has completely stopped traffic, and several carts with bales of cotton have come to a standstill near Ntonda. This is a deplorable state of affairs. We understand Mr. Fletcher has been sent to repair the road, but it is quite evident that the cotton must suffer serious damage while exposed to this weather.

Mining & General Supplies Co., Ltd.,

6, CROSBY SQUARE, LONDON, E.C.

SEE DISPLAYED ADVERTISEMENT IN FEBRUARY 27th ISSUE.

Congo Free State News.

(From our Special Correspondent.)

BRUSSELS, March 9.

The "Albertville."

This fine steamer returned on Tuesday from the Congo with sixty passengers, amongst whom was the Vice-Governor of the Free State, Monsieur Fuchs. The steamer, which brought a cargo of 860 tons, experienced very bad weather during the whole of the journey.

Death of Monsieur Laurent.

A gloom was thrown over the journey of the *Albertville* by the death at sea, from pernicious malaria, of M. Laurent, the well-known savant and botanist. The patient's condition rapidly became worse, in spite of every care and attention on the part of Dr. Waerseghers, of the nephew of Mr. Laurent, of Mr. Brandel (general assistant-secretary), and of Lieutenants Mary and Braeckman. The patient died without recovering consciousness. When the news of the death became known the passengers were filled with consternation. Mr. Fuchs, the Vice-Governor of the Congo, and M Sparrow, the Captain of the *Albertville*, established the fact of the death and transacted the legal formalities. At a quarter to nine the ship's bell began tolling, and the passengers lined up silently on deck. The Captain and the officers were in full uniform. On the stroke of nine the bier, draped with a flag, was brought on deck by the sailors. Mr. Fuchs, in a touching speech, recalled how the deceased had been his father's scholar and his own personal friend. After the speech, Captain Sparrow recited a short prayer and the coffin was committed to the deep.

The Laurent Mission.

The results of the Laurent mission are bri... numerous documents on board, from which J (the nephew of the learned botanist) will draw report. Among the plants brought back by Mr plants which is very little known. The interi branches of this plant serve as a dwelling for t

Mission of the L.S.T.M.

The mission under Dr. Bowden, in connectior School of Tropical Medicine, is at present repo The members are delighted with their journey s and also their reception en route.

Mrs. French Sheldon.

This famous American lady-explorer i ... now at Stanleyville, and is studying the rubber industry ... spot, particularly the system of collection and preparation ... produce before despatch to Europe.

Wireless Waves in the Congo.

The new wireless installation between Banana and Ambrizette was worked successfully for the first time on February 6 by its installator, an Austrian engineer named Benton.

An Excellent Work.

La Tribune Congolaise has just issued a comprehensive volume, "Leopold II. et le Congo," by Consul Boillot-Robert, which is particularly welcome at the present juncture, giving as it does a brilliant record by pen and picture of the splendid work performed by the administration in the opening up of this great equatorial territory.

MR. CASEMENT'S ALLEGATIONS.

The Marquis Bosco has concluded his inquiry into the report of the British Consul at Boma as to the administration of the Congo State, and says that he absolutely contradicts the Consul's allegations.

French Africa.

(From our Special Correspondent.)

PARIS, March 10.

Commissary-General of the French Congo.

Monsieur Emile Gentil, the newly-appointed Commissary-General of the French Congo, which has just been politically transformed in regard to its administration, will leave for Brazzaville on March 15 next. On his arrival he will make a long tour of inspection throughout the region under his direct command. He will be accompanied by Staff-Captain Gouraud, of the Chad Military Department.

Sanitary Condition of French Colonies.

Chief Medical Officer M. Kermorgant has just furnished a detailed report on the sanitary condition of the French colonies for 1902. Yellow fever and cholera were, it appears, responsible for a somewhat heavy mortality among French colonial troops in the Ivory Coast, the Sudan, French Indies, and in Madagascar. M. Kermorgant curtly remarks that if strict measures be not taken at once leprosy will shortly make its appearance in the metropolis!

A Trip from Brazzaville to Alexandria.

M. Pierre, manager of the Compagnie des Sultanats du Haut Oubanghi, has just completed a somewhat remarkable tour. The itinerary was as follows:—Brazzaville, Bangui, Bangasso, Rafaï, Zemio, Djema, Dem-Ziber, Waou (Anglo-Egyptian post), Tewfikieh, Kabac (of Marchand renown), Wady Halfa, Philoe-Assuan, Cairo, Alexandria, Marseilles. Total distance, 7,000 kilometres accomplished in eight months!

...ormous damage ...ean lives were ...nishing vanilla, ...us. Water is Comores oxen The islands who make both ...ial year.

...colonial stock, of some fifteen ...: for instance, ...pital, the Compagnie des Caoutchoucs de la Casamance enters into liquidation, the Société de Recherches de Madagascar has been dissolved, and so on throughout the French colonies. But the total losses incurred do not reach by one-thousandth part the shocking losses in the jungle market.

Important African Patents.

I recently referred to a new German patent which permitted of a much larger extraction of palm oil, and at a low cost—a process which could be easily manipulated by the native. The palm-nut contains some 22 per cent. of oil, of which 7 per cent. only is actually extracted by native processes and about 10 per cent. by European methods. By the new German process, known as the Haake Oil Extractor, it is said that as much as 18 per cent. of the oil can be extracted and that by the native; the machine being as easy to manage as it is ingenious. Another machine about to be introduced into Africa is bound to render immense services to the cotton-growing industry of the Dark Continent. I refer to a certain cotton gin now on the market.

Camels for the St. Louis Exhibition.

The *Depêche Tunisienne* states that seventeen superb camels were embarked on the 20th ult. on board the Italian steamer *Caridd̀i* for Naples, where they will be transferred to the cargo boat *Lombardia*, which will be entirely loaded with exhibits for St. Louis. These animals have been bought by Mr. Zitoun, superintendent of the Jerusalem Exhibition Company, in the region of Kairouan.

A series of letters written by people who knew Johnny.

W Roberts　　　　　　　　　　　　　　　　　　　　　　　　Salcombe, Devon

I first remember Mr Benton, "Uncle Johnny" to me, about 1910 – 1912, when as a boy at Pinkney's Green, I, with others, helped to hold down his large kite. This he flew at great height to test air currents etc. Later I went to see his hangar at Chalvey, nr Slough, where he had a plane. He showed me this and let me go for a short ride with him, but only a short run with him, a foot or so off the ground, then he shut off the engine and landed. He would not go any higher as it was too close to the Sewage Works and he was afraid of landing in it (!). When the 1914 – 18 war started he turned all his ideas over to the War Office. Most of his inventions were used on the early planes, which enabled the War Office to catch up on the Germans who were much in advance of us. In later years he was very bitter about this, because someone else got recognition for his work. I expect you will wonder why I write War Office instead of Air Ministry, this was not in existence in those days.

Another idea of his was when there was a big shortage of shells because something which was used to pack the explosive in could not be obtained. He thought up an idea for this which he made in waxed paper, and took it up to the War Office. After much waiting he managed to get an interview, and after explaining about his idea, he was told to put it down on a side table. Still the outcry went on about a shortage of shells so he made a second attempt to get things going. He again visited the War Office, to find his pattern was still where he had been told to leave it.

Shortly afterwards he was told that his idea was accepted, and that "formers" would be sent to him to make them on. His partner, Mr Allen's wife, found a short piece of cycle–frame tubing about 12 inches long at Timberlakes Cycle Works at Maidenhead which was the exact size. She cut this into short lengths, and got a number of girls making them. When she got the go–ahead from the War Office she sent them on to where they had to go, only to have them returned, with a letter to say they could not be correct, as the formers had not yet been dispatched. However when the "formers" came, they found that they were exactly the same size, so they sent one of the cases again and received a letter from the War Office thanking them for their prompt delivery.

In the Second World War, when the magnetic mine was so troublesome to shipping, he said to me, "Why that's simple", and described an idea to me. I said, "Why not send it up to the Admiralty", but after his last treatment he said "no" emphatically. I finally persuaded him to send it, I believe to a friend, Captain Medlicott, MP for Norfolk. Shortly afterwards a big splash was made in the papers with the headlines, "Magnetic Mine Conquered". There is no doubt that he was a very clever man, with a brain years ahead of the times. I think Captain Medlicott tried to get his ideas going but to what extent I am not quite certain. Although all this happened a long time ago, I am sure some mention of his achievements would not be amiss.

W Roberts　　　　　　　　　　　　　　　　　　　　　　　　　　　*14th July 1971*

E S Spackman

Malta Green
Grittleton
Chippenham, Wilts
5th July 1974

The name of our farm at Chalvey was Manor Farm. Eton College bought it from my mother. I am enclosing a tracing from a 1947 one inch National Grid map number 158, very small scale, but it will give you an idea of the position of the hangar and flying field.

Mr Benton came to Chalvey in 1907, put up the hangar and had the use of the field. Mr Allen gave up his camera manufacturing business, he made brass bound wooden cameras, they cycled from Maidenhead every day and built the aeroplane entirely by hand, even the propellors, built up from planks glued together and carved, the blades were about ten inches across. The struts were hollow, the tail planes and ailerons were controlled by a joy stick. The machine with twin props and double main wings was made about 1910 – 1911 and I believe never flew, but I saw the Moth type machine fly about a mile to the next farm in 1912. Mr Benton was seated in it. In 1917 Mr Benton closed the hangar and started a munitions factory in Maidenhead employing a lot of girls making cardboard containers for explosives in shells, making the jigs on a four inch Drummond lathe I still possess. After the war he made jewellery, living then at "Philberds", Lane End, High Wycombe; Mrs Allen, his housekeeper and her invalid son sharing this.

I let the hangar after the war to an amateur flyer who had a Moth and a Monospar.

28th July 1974

Seated under the petrol tank, I had a brief hop, finishing up in a hedge in about 1913, I was eleven then. Since then I got my pilot's licence (No 7421) at Reading in 1934 in a Miles Hawk, but found it too expensive to keep up.

ESS

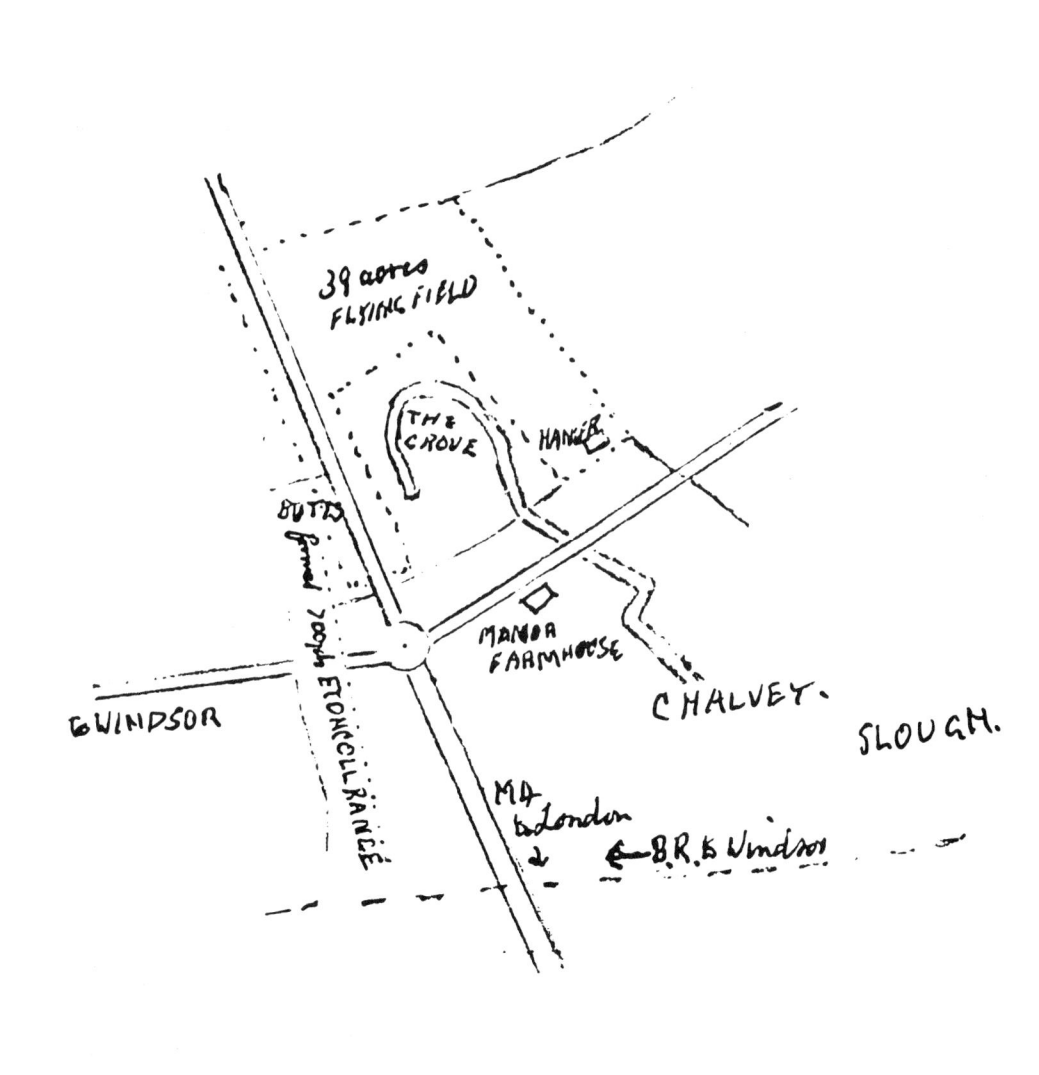

Plan of Flying Field

Lady Medlicott New Malden, Surrey
29th September 1977

I have been handed your letter and request for any papers relating to the work of John Benton.

I am more than sorry that I have no papers, either at my home, or in my late husband's records.

I wish that I could help you, but all I have are very warm memories and numberless recollections of a loving and very remarkable man, whose work was woefully overlooked during his life time, owing, I must admit, partly to the complete chaos in which his study was kept – only may I add to other people's eyes, he kept track of everything! He was a wonderfully kind, considerate man and was mourned by many "small" people who had known his kindness.

I am sorry not to have been of any help,
Sincerely,
Helen Medlicott

John B Allaway 17th June 1971

I last saw "Uncle" Johnny Benton at the beginning of the war, about 1940, but prior to that I had seen him almost weekly on his visits to friends at Tilehurst. I was only about 17 years old when I last saw him – just as I was about to enter the RAF, but from the age of eight I had worried him with my questions about his early experiences with man–lifting kites and his activities with Marconi's in the field of wireless. He had a large scrapbook containing pictures and articles cut from newspapers and although I cannot be sure of the date I remember that he was credited with staying aloft for some three hours in a kite which was hauled aloft by a steam winch which was anchored to the ground in the middle of the common at Pinkney's Green. The steam engine, which was marked on the side, was made by the Reading Iron Company and I saw it and coveted it in his shed on many occasions. I remember that he said that the reason he was successful in staying aloft was because he designed the winch gear to heave the kite along to get it aloft and then to apply a reciprocating motion to the hawser. He always reckoned he could have stayed aloft longer if his stomach had allowed it!

He was retained by Marconi's to evolve a method of taking aerial wire aloft and in this was very successful and he spent some time with the firm on the Isle of Wight.

The engine for the aeroplanes he built was a flat four cylinder air–cooled thing that he had converted from low–tension ignition to magneto.

John B Allaway

John B Allaway **16th March 1989**

I knew J F B so very well when I was a little boy, and always listened to all his tales of his youth. I knew him because he had a lifelong friendship with the Roberts family, who were related to the Drew family of Reading, and as a small boy I was often taken to the Roberts's house. J F B used to have a big scrapbook which had a lot of cuttings that had been published in "The Maidenhead Advertiser" and there were some photographs of him going up in a man–lifting kite during the experiments in wireless transmissions to America. I seem to remember that he said that he was doing the work at Poldu in Cornwall. I believe that there is a picture in a book about man–lifting kites that was published a few years ago, Uncle Johnny is the one in the "gondola".

22nd March 1989

The engine that was in the garage at Lane End, made by the Reading Iron Company was the steam engine that he used to keep his kite aloft, the engine for the aeroplane was a flat four cylinder thing that he converted from low tension ignition to magneto.

16th April 1989

I expect that you know the connection between the Roberts family and Uncle Johnny, but to recap I will tell it as I heard it all. Apparently Wally Roberts lived at Pinkney's Green, and as a small boy delivered milk to most of the houses in the area, the dairy being owned by a man called Lansbury, and it was while he was delivering the milk that he got to know J F B who was making "interesting things" in his shed, and was able to help after school doing mundane things like lifting and cleaning. The result was that a long friendship grew up, and when Wally Roberts got himself married and moved over to Reading, he continued to see J F B on a regular basis. Wally's wife Florence, was a Miss Drew before her marriage, the Drew's being very well–known as grocery wholesalers in Reading. In later years the Roberts' moved to Tilehurst, just outside Reading, and started up a chicken farm, and at the same time kept bees in quite large quantity, selling honey and eggs at the door, but mainly selling the eggs to the catering industry. The chicken farm was a big enterprise for those days – thousands of eggs being transported all over the country, and it was to this end that the egg carrying invention that Uncle Johnny made was used to such great effect.

Uncle Johnny was at the chicken farm almost daily, and used to tend the bees. I did not know whether he had any interest in the farm in a financial way, but I think he really came over as a friendly gesture to give as much help as he could. This would have been about 1937/8. He had started on his "healing" circuit at this time, and had quite a few patients in the Reading area, and used to go to the Reading Spiritualist Church on Thursdays.

John B Allaway

A History of the Flying Field at Chalvey

The Windsor area was the centre for amateur pioneer aviation before the First World War and many people arrived there to try their hand at this exciting new activity. It is not unreasonable to think that these early budding flyers were eager to provide entertainment for the Royal Family and thus gain their patronage! As it turned out the outbreak of war changed that approach more abruptly and dramatically than anything else could possibly have done.

The airfield at Chalvey was originally on the Great or Big Pasture which was a 35 acre area on Manor Farm. This was owned by a Philip Headington who sold it to the Spackman family around 1910, old Walter Spackman then let the 35 acres of Big Meadow to John F Benton on the 19th June 1911 until the end of December for £22–10–0. The agreement drawn up between them allowed J F B to put up a hangar and use the field for flying aeroplanes and also agreed that Walter could harvest the grass that grew on it each summer!

This arrangement continued until 1917, for Johnny's last aeroplane that he built was still in the hangar at that time. Walter's son E S Spackman then let the field to an "amateur flyer who kept a D H Moth and a Monospar there", ESS did his flying at Reading and got his licence in 1934 in a Miles Hawk.

In the 20's and 30's the field was used by the Jackaman family who lived at the junction of Ledgers Road and the Bath Road. At this time the farm was owned by Eton College who bought it from E S Spackman's mother. The Jackaman's flew two aeroplanes – a two seater open cockpit Moth and a four seater cabin aeroplane, they used to fly to Bognor or the Norfolk coast for a swim before breakfast. On return they circled their house low as a signal and someone would come to the field and pick them up.

Michael Bayley remembers an air display there in 1937, now part of the land is built up and called The Grove, wonder how many people living there are aware of the historic past of the place!

An Agreement

this day between Walter Spackman, of Manor Farm, Chalvey, Slough, of the one part, and John F. Benton Esq, of Ford Cottage, Pinkneys Green, Maidenhead, Berks, of the other part. The said Walter Spackman agrees to allow the said John F. Benton Esq the privilege of using the field called the Great, or Big Pasture, a part of the said Manor Farm, Chalvey Slough as a trial aviation ground from the nineteenth of June One Thousand, nine hundred and eleven, to the thirty first of December, One Thousand, nine hundred and eleven, for the sum of twenty two pounds, ten shillings, sterling, the said amount to be paid to the said Walter Spackman by the said John F. Benton Esq on the signature of the said agreement. The aeroplanes to be tried by the said John F. Benton Esq to be wholly or partly his own property. The said John F. Benton Esq to have the privilege of erecting a shed or hangar in the said field for the purpose of housing his aeroplane or aeroplanes, and to have the privilege of removing the said shed or hangar at the end of the above time or at any time previous to the above time. The said John F. Benton Esq to be wholly responsible for any damage caused by, through, or as the result of the use of the said aeroplanes, either to the property or person of the said Walter Spackman or to the property or person of any other person whatsoever. Should John F. Benton Esq wish to continue using the said field after the thirty first of December One Thousand nine hundred and eleven the said Walter Spackman agrees to let the said field to him on the same terms as above.

Signed { Walter Spackman
John Frederick Benton.

Witness.

Michael H H Bayley   **24th May 1989**
                                                                                             ARIBA, Dipl Arch Oxford

    I know the field used as an aerodrome in Chalvey well, and enclose a copy of an old field map of the area with the field in The Grove marked and the approximate position of the hangar marked with a cross. The Bath Road (A4) is coloured yellow and the Windsor Road green, so you can get your bearings from a modern map.

    The field was part of Manor Farm, Chalvey, which in about 1910 belonged to Philip Headington, who in a fit of patriotism sold up and joined the army in 1915. It was Spackman's who took it over, and I think it must have been old Mr Spackman who learned to fly, it was obviously J F B's hangar and airfield that the Jackaman family took over and where an air display was staged in about 1937.

Philip Headington, Esq

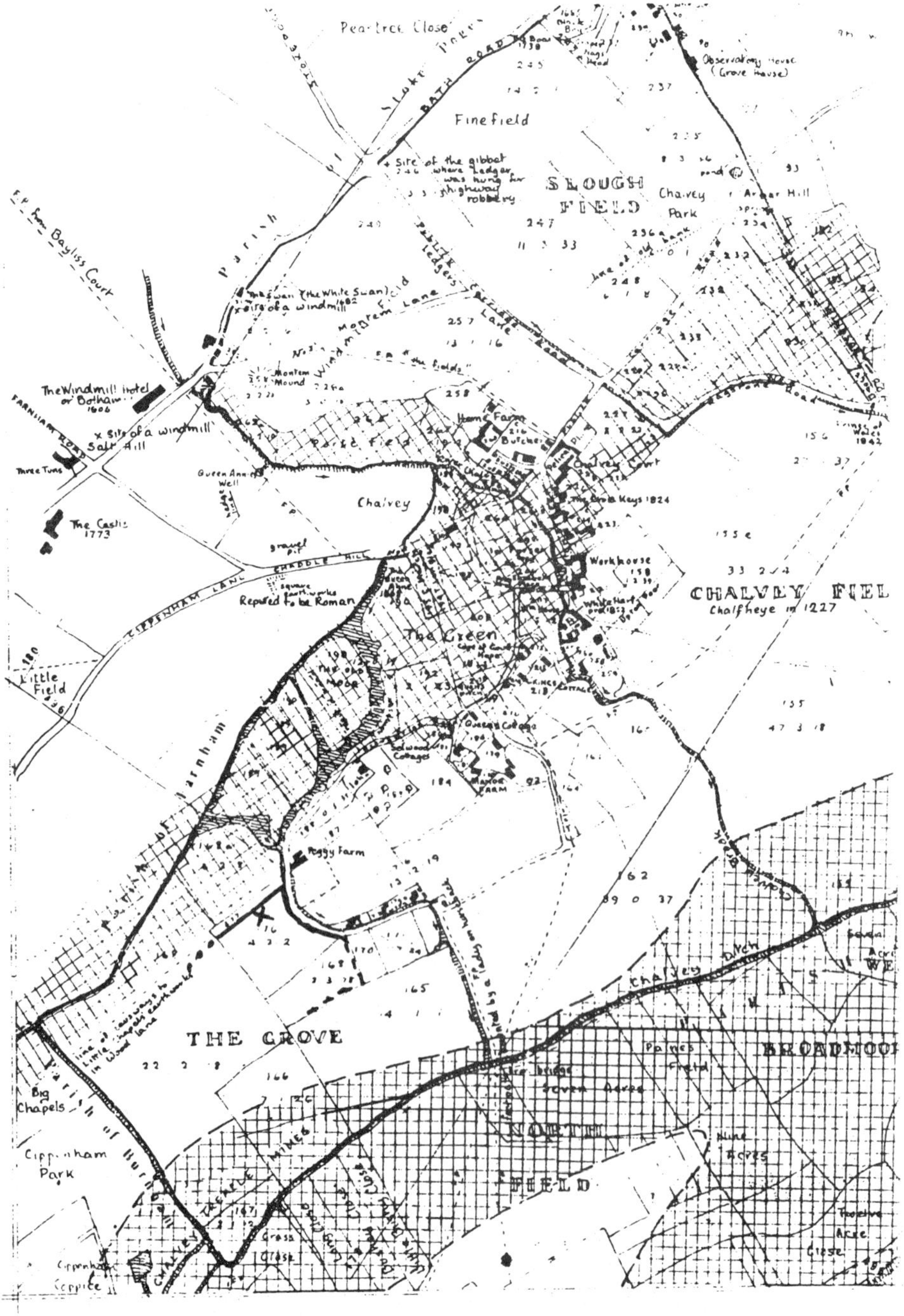

Peartree Close
Stoke Poges
Bath Road
Observatory House (Grove House)
Finefield
Site of the gibbet where Ledger was hung for highway robbery
SLOUGH FIELD
Chalvey Park
Arbour Hill
Parish
Site of a windmill
Montem Lane
Montem Mound
The Windmill Hotel or Botham 1606
Farnham Road
x Site of a windmill
Salt Hill
Three Tuns
Queen Anne's Well
Home Farm
Chalvey
The Cross Keys 1824
The Castle 1773
gravel pit
Chaddle Hill
Cippenham Lane
Reputed to be Roman
Workhouse
CHALVEY FIEL
Chalfheye in 1227
The Green
Little Field
Queens Cottage
Manor Farm
Peggy Farm
THE GROVE
Chalvey Ditch
Paines Field
Seven Acres
NORTH FIELD
BROADMOO
Big Chapels
Cippenham Park
Nine Acres
Cross Close
Cippenham Coppice

Maidenhead's "Air Car"

The conquest of the air is not altogether a latter-day craze, as many people fancy. It is a problem which has occupied the minds of men for centuries, but only during the last few years has anything approaching a triumph over the elements been achieved by the inventive genius of man. Who, however can truly say that the successes attained are complete, since so many lives have been lost in acquiring the art of flight by machine? It is still a very hazardous undertaking. There are numerous types of flying machines, more or less imperfect. By practical experience theories are corrected, and a higher degree of efficiency in construction and manipulation of flying machines is obtained, and it is the general belief that it is now merely a matter of time when people will be able to travel from place to place in absolute safety. The producing of a machine in which the possibilities of disaster will be practically reduced to an improbability, is being attempted by many interested in aerial flight. Mr John Benton, an Australian by birth, has been solely engaged in Maidenhead during the last eleven months, in an effort to present a really successful machine. Last June permission was obtained by him from the Maidenhead Corporation to erect a corrugated iron shed in a meadow adjoining Green Lane, where, with the assistance of Mr Allen, of York Road, and another assistant, they have worked assiduously until now his Air Car is completed. The work of construction was actually finished on Good Friday, and the aeroplane, or as Mr Benton calls it, the "Air Car", was run out of the shed to the meadow into the full light of day. The first trial run, as recorded in the "Advertiser", took place on Thursday week last, and proved eminently satisfactory. The machine is not extraordinary in character, as, for instance, is Col Davidson's Gyropter at Taplow, but its method of control is unique in that the aviator claims to be able very easily to govern the movements of the aeroplane.

A lucid explanation and demonstration of the means of control of the "Air Car" was kindly given by Mr Benton to a representative of the Advertiser during the course of an interview. Mounting the car, he said

"You see the first thing a person would notice is that the aviator naturally drops into all the things which automatically regulate the machine. When flying should the "car" heel over to one side it would be the natural impulse for the aviator to lean in the opposite direction. That motion would cause the seat to move and at the same time force the connections to deflect the wing tips and thus bring the car to an even keel. The feet rest on pedals with which the rudders are controlled in exactly the same way as the rudders of a rowing boat, only that one presses with either the left or right foot according to the direction one desires to travel. Then by the right hand is a lever which if pushed to the front causes the plane to point downwards and the "air car" to descend, while the reverse action is necessary for ascent. The left hand also naturally reaches to a wheel, which, when turned to the right, heightens the angle of the front plane and so increases the speed, and, if turned to the left causes a decrease in the speed irrespective of the rate the propellors are revolving."

"Yes, it's all very simple" I remarked. "That is so", said Mr Benton, "although the structure is intricate. In teaching a pupil how to control this machine, I would impress upon him to do what instinct told him to do and all would be well. Watch this! Now say the machine is rising too much it would be natural to press down. Well all that would be required would be to press the right hand lever forward and the planes fore and aft would lower". Suiting the action to the word, Mr Benton put the lever forward and the planes altered their angle immediately. "Then", he went on, "when you are proceeding as you desire you would leave go of the lever which locks automatically". "You have doubtless often noticed when a bird is flying", proceeded Mr Benton, "it will change its course apparently when there is no reason for doing so. That is in all probability because it has met a gust of wind and in order to right itself it swerves to the right to fly directly into the wind. With this machine, however, if a gust of wind were to strike it it would not be necessary for the operator to change the course and face the wind. If the gust of wind struck the machine for instance, from the left, the "car" would heel over and the natural balancing of the body would cause the wing tips on the opposite side to be raised automatically, thus bringing it to an even keel. If the gust of wind were extremely heavy then the airman would use both foot and body which would operate the rudder and wing tips and the course desired would be maintained. This is how in this machine there would be an advantage over the bird".

"Now the next thing we will talk about", continued Mr Benton, "is the engine. At the back of the seat is a button which is used to switch on or off the electric current used with the engine. Reaching over (and one can do so without causing the lever on the back of the seat to act) one can reach the throttle and govern the power of the motor, which is the make of the New Engine Company of London, and is therefore British. The fact that it is a two cycle engine at once distinguishes it from an ordinary motor car engine, for instead of there being an explosion every other revolution, as with a motor car engine, there is an explosion at every revolution. That means the engine is more powerful. The lubrication to the bearings is forced, the pressure being about 15 lbs to the spare inch and that results in all the moving parts of the engine running on a film of oil".

"Why is there a space between the spot where you sit and the engine?", I asked. "Oh, that," Mr Benton replied, "is where I will be able to seat two other passengers which this "air car" is designed to carry. Beside that just below can be placed another tank for petrol, to be used on runs of a very long duration". In answer to another question, the inventor of the "car" said: "A great feature of the machine is the under-chassis which is mounted on springs – the whole machine is really mounted on springs, which are extremely resilient. When I had my first run down the meadow what astonished me most was the perfect smoothness with which the machine ran over all the mounds. I could only feel a slight swaying motion, when I really expected to be almost jerked out of my seat. That was a proof that the "car" was slightly lifting, although I was only travelling at the rate of about between 10 to

15 miles an hour. So even with that small rate of speed there was a considerable lifting power with the planes. "How does the "car" act when you first start?", I asked. "Unlike most other machines" he said, "my flying machine does not require holding back at the start. The moment the propellors are started the head of the machine dips down on the front wooden skids and then rises gracefully". Further Mr Benton explained that the main weight of the machine was supported fore and aft by moveable bi-planes and quite apart from the extra amount of lifting surface by the bi-plane system adopted there was a great length of "cutting edge", which counts for a great deal in aerial flight. The whole of the machine, with the exception of the NEC engine, the propeller shafts and wheel brackets, was made at Mr Benton's works, he has called this establishment: "Green Lane Engineering Works". The propeller shafts were made by Mr Norkett (Maidenhead) to Mr Benton's design, while the wheel brackets were made by Mr Thos Timberlake, Maidenhead. The machine can, therefore be said to be of British and Maidenhead production. The machine is lightly built – it only weighs one thousand pounds – but is of remarkable strength.

Something must now be said about the inventor of the machine. By birth he can claim to be an Australian, being born in the year 1882 at a little township known as Corowa deep in the Outback. A few years later Mr Benton's parents came to England and took up residence in London. As a boy young Benton went to Westminster City School, and from about the year 1896 became deeply fascinated in the problem of flight through air, and his one source of play was the construction of model aeroplanes made from the staves of old Venetian blinds given to him for the purpose by the caretaker of the Mansion in Victoria Street, in which was his home. "A married sister of mine, Mrs Harker, who is well-known in Maidenhead", said Mr Benton, "while on a recent visit to London, met the old caretaker, whose first remark was, "Is your brother flying now?", and he was delighted to learn that my real flying machine was constructed". "In those school-boy days of mine," he continued, "the propelling force was electricity, and the machine was forced through the air by flapping wings, as those of a bird. My experiments, unfortunately, were stopped through my having to go to college at South Kensington, where I qualified as an electrical engineer. Upon completion of my studies at college, I joined Marconi's Wireless Company, and while in their service travelled over England and Ireland, installing wireless apparatus, but chiefly the work was of an experimental nature. Later I went to the Congo to set up certain stations and establish wireless communication, which was the first work of its kind to be done successfully in Africa. The electrical arrangements at those African stations (Mr Benton explained) were quite novel. The masts used were over 200 feet high. On the Congo the phenomena were quite new and much difficulty was experienced owing to the local electrical disturbances which had to be overcome by the Marconi system. It was not an unusual thing, either, during the dispatch and receipt of messages, for the electrical sparks from the apparatus due to these disturbances to be over an inch in length. Mr Benton was extremely happy in Africa. He travelled through delightfully picturesque country to the town of Matadi and on to the Stanley Falls.

At the former place the river, which is in certain parts from between 12 to 14 miles wide, narrows down to a width of about 800 feet. The force of water consequent upon the narrowing of the river causes eddies of an extremely dangerous character, being fully eight feet deep. At Matadi (which means town of stone) the sight of rushing water was exceedingly refreshing, for the heat reflected by the stone upon which one walked was almost unbearable. While in the Congo Mr Benton had access to a large quantity of bamboo and, therefore, during leisure hours, perfected his ideas of aeroplane construction by working on the plans already formulated, and gradually brought the plan of his present "air car" to an issue. In 1905 Mr Benton returned to London, where he spent a period of two years in the work of calculations and the plans for an aeroplane, and in the construction of working models. In 1908 he came to Maidenhead and rented a house on Maidenhead thicket where he carried out numerous experiments with his models. When the models acted perfectly our aviator was anxious to construct his aeroplane. As stated above, he obtained sanction from the Corporation and had a shed erected in a meadow in Green Lane. "I wanted a mechanic who could not only do work in wood, but also in iron and steel. Through Mr Upson JP, the chemist, I heard of Mr Allen and obtained his services, and I am more than satisfied with his work; he has been the greatest help to me".

From time to time during the building of his aeroplanes, Mr Benton holds "open days" at his flying field in Chalvey and he invites members of the public to walk into the hangar and inspect the work going on. Ever mindful of the welfare of his customers he displays a large warning notice pointing out the danger of approaching the "Air Car" when the engine is running. The boys from Eton College are frequent and enthusiastic visitors.

Mr Benton is a gentleman of rather small stature, and is modest in the extreme. He has a strong willpower and does not know how to spell "failure", while he is possessed of that nerve, coolness, rapidity of thought and action, and keenness in calculation and resourcefulness which are indispensable in the real aviator.

The townspeople of Maidenhead are anxiously waiting for Mr Benton to achieve the success in aerial navigation which has been his life's dream and work, and in his enterprise we wish him the best of success.

Wednesday 17th May 1911

Accident to Mr Benton's Air Car

Aeroplane to be housed for two months

Mr John F Benton, who, during the past few weeks has been engaged in a series of trial "runs" with his "air car" in a meadow in Green Lane, Maidenhead, on Saturday evening, while further experimenting with his aeroplane, met with an accident of a minor character, which resulted in damage to the forepart of the aeroplane. Curiously enough, the aviator had decided that this should be the last trial that he would make with the "car" for a period of two months, as the grass in the field is required for hay. The machine was taken out of the shed in which it is berthed at about seven o'clock in the evening, and when all was in readiness the propellors were set in motion and the "car" lightly skimming over the surface of the field, travelled at a rate of between 10 and 15 miles an hour. Mr Benton piloted the aeroplane near the Green Lane hedge and shut off the engine as the other side of the field was reached. The "car" flew clean over the ditch, but the impetus gained carried it too far and a collision with the hedge at the end of the field was inevitable. The front skids were smashed and the central part of the back edge of the lower fore–plane was damaged, owing to the bending of one of the steel stays. Beyond this, however, the "car" is intact. Mr Benton escaped injury. The damaged parts will be replaced quite easily. The two months which will elapse before the "car" will be able to be taken out again will be occupied by Mr Benton in making further alterations which will greatly improve the craft. These improvements are the result of the experience gained by the trials in the meadow.

1911

Descriptive Specification of
Benton VI Variable Speed Biplane

John F Benton
Maidenhead, Berkshire
July 1915

The wings are built up with hollowed pine and ash mainspars. The back ash spar is universally hinged and the front pine spar hinged at body junction by specially designed and "fool proof" unions which prevent constraint being accidentally set up in the wing when being assembled. The wing segments are of silver spruce, parany, and alder three ply ensuring permanency of shape and rigidity, wings are at a positive dihedral angle 176°. Top wing is longer and wider than the bottom wing and wings widen towards the centre which increases the angle of attack towards the roots and has the aerodynamic effect of increasing the aspect ratio above the estimated mean for the given wing surface. Wing tips are rounded and washed out. Internal wire stays are of heavy gauge. Variable speed and lateral balance is effected by flexors as per provisional patent specification and diagram sheet no 3 herewith. The supporting surface is calculated sufficient with these flexors fully washed out for the maximum HP available. With flexors brought into normal position greatly reduced speed is obtained without altering the flying keel of the machine or change of altitude and with the engine throttled. With 35/40 NEC two stroke watercooled engine range of speed with fourth machine was 33 to 50 mph. Loss of altitude when turning is much reduced by the compensating rocker (re diagram sheet 3) which decreases the resistance of the outside and faster moving wing tip for a given bank. Wing stanchions are all fitted with universal joints of special mechanical and "fool proof" design are interchangeable and stanchions are all of the same standard length. Built up of hollowed white pine, glued and taped at bridging. Section is long streamline. Stanchions with their universal joints are removed by one screw–eye top and bottom which cannot be lost as they form the ends of the fore and aft stays and are all (including these stays) interchangeable and distinctly recognisable from the main stays. When the machine is assembled stanchions lock themselves automatically in place apart from this screw–eye. The adoption of universal joints on wing spar roots and stanchions prevents accidental constraint and makes the machine very readily set up and aligned. The tail fuselage is built up entirely of 3 ply panels and silver spruce mains, absolutely rigid and very light without any internal stays to set up. It is streamlined practically without discontinuety to the trailing edge of the elevators. Tail is non–lifting and streamlined in every way, it is carried by 1" x 1" mahogany middle spar, tapered 3" to 1" pine leading spar and two oval steel distance pieces. The tail skid is universally hinged at its fulcrum and its arm is carried by rubber springs to the ends of a transverse sliding steel bar which projects about 3" from each side of the three–ply tail and is coupled by separate and adjusted cables to the rudder foot control lever, and comes into play for ground steering at a given point. The tail fuselage is readily detachable from the body by channel plates. Weight of tail fuselage complete with empennage about 70 lbs. Wheel system see Patent No 12375/1911 appended hereto. I have used this on the last three machines with unfailing success. It takes up every kind of landing and travelling shock and in conjunction with the tail skid enables a nicety of ground steering and enables one to alight in very confined spaces. The life of this arrangement is practically unlimited since no direct wear and tear comes on any of the four springs. Side shocks and motion are most interestingly absorbed by this system; the machine "floats" from its wheels. When in flight the head resistance is reduced by the spring coming into line through relief from load. The chassis is built up as a separate unit and standardised. Photograph marked "chassis" herewith, it is intended to show means of readily detaching same as a whole from the body. The pine lightening bridge shewn comes away with the chassis from beneath the body longitudinals. Struts are all built up of hollowed white pine glued and taped at bridging. Sections are long and streamlined and carefully aligned to the direction of travel. Skids are mahogany and width of skid track 6 ft. Complete weight is very low for robust design 100 lbs. Head resistance is extremely low. The body, like the tail fuselage is built up of three ply panels. It is reinforced by inside stays and carries with it the 2 ft top central portion of the wings on four permanent central stanchions as shewn on tracing sheet 2 herewith. The observer sits immediately behind the engine section and above petrol tanks which are designed without any bottom taps or unions. The pilot section is behind the observer and the centre of gravity. The engine is carried inside the front section of the body and geared by double chain to counter shaft above it, carrying a 9 ft $8^1/2''$ tractor of big pitch. The propellor is of special and careful design with conversion efficiency. Shape of each 6" blade section is accurately calculated and its dimensions are directly deduced from the speed, thrust and energy absorbed and not arrived at empirically. Propellors are balanced to a nicety. Weight of complete machine including in this instance a 35/40 hp watercooled engine weighing 223 lbs and its fittings – 910 lbs.

S—A
611
1915

Benton VI 100 hp   John F Benton

Variable Speed Tractor Biplane   Maidenhead, Berkshire

November 1915

The chief features of Benton Biplane B VI to which I have been asked to make special reference:–

I   Means of varying the flying speed and

II   a   Shock absorbing system on travelling wheels together with

      b   Shock absorbing steerable tail skid

III   The wings are so constructed that the angle of incidence and camber decrease from the centre of the wing tips. A definite amount of the rear wing "suds" is hinged as shewn in sheet I and diagramatically in sheet 3 and is controlled by cables passing through the rocker shown in sheet 3 to the worm wheel half way up the control column. By letting out this worm the wing tips are washed out in camber and angle of attack, the engine revs rise and the machine flies faster. The range of speed in a former biplane B4 engined with 35 hp two stroke watercooled NEC was 33 to 52 mph and weight of machine 910 lbs plus pilot and fuel. My experiments have conclusively shewn that it is wrong to apply this system to the centre of the wings the effect being that its efficiency falls off from the wing tips inwards becoming impractical beyond a certain point. The reasons are because:–

    a   It tends to give rise to an unequally distributed, distorted and produces eddies near the centre absorbing energy.

    b   The greater the angle of attack and camber at the wing tips the greater are the cyclical losses there and

    c   It produces transverse instability.

To give a differential movement to the ailerons the rocker through which the aforesaid wing tip cables pass is fixed above a quadrant. This rotates about a vertical axis and is controlled by cables passing to the hand wheel at the top of the control column. The arms of the rocker are crossed and disposed in the manner shewn, so that when the quadrant is rotated by the control wheel whereas that end of the rocker which tightens the wing tip cable moves nearly about a dead centre the other end produces a maximum amount of slack to the other wing tip cable. In this way a minimum amount of resistance is introduced against the outer and faster moving wing tip when turning. By a further development of the wings, mention of which I append hereto, I am able to decrease the actual wing area while flying, and retaining the foregoing am able to make it noticeably more effective.

The shock absorbing device is fully described in the patent Specification 12375 of 1911 appended hereto and is shown plainly in the accompanying photograph (marked B3) of my third machine. I have made many rough landings with this system and never come to grief. I have never so much as buckled a wheel and have used it on and through all the experimental work of four machines. When flying, the rubber springs which form a lozenge of which the axle and skid are diagonals come automatically into the same plane with the axle producing a minimum resistance. If two wheels only are to be used as in B6 the inside wheels are replaced by a telescopic axle piece. The weight of the absorbers is seven pounds per set, there is no direct contact with the springs which are only in tension and the life is therefore that of the covered rubber, say three years which I find allows a good margin of safety. The springs are a commercial article and machines can be readily fitted withthe system. About two feet from the tail end of the fuselage (see sheet 2) a 3/4 inch steel tube projects three inches from each side of the three–ply wood fuselage. This tube slides in an outer steel tube built into the fuselage and control cables pass from there to the rudder foot control lever. These cables are quite distinct from the rudder cables and not connected to the rudder. The two projecting ends of the steel tube are connected direct by light rubber springs in tension to the top of the trailing skid arm. The skid is universally hinged to its fulcrum. Directional motion can therefore be imparted to the trailing skid, the vertical and side shocks being taken up by the springs. This skid arrangement together with my resilient wheel system has enabled me to take off from and come down on to indifferent and rough ground and to steer away from hedges etc, when after landing the headway is reduced (and there is no propellor stream) to an extent that makes the rudder useless. I have been able to carry out my experiments from confined meadows.

Appendix

The new Benton wing is so constructed that its area can be reduced by about one third (and restored) while flying. Simultaneously the aspect ratio is somewhat increased and the centre of pressure automatically kept in the original position. I am able to retain the B6 variable wing tips and enhance their aerodynamic effectiveness. The mechanical arrangements are very simple and I am able to fit wings of this new type to existing machines. The extra weight in a 43 ft span machine is approximately 65 lbs. The connections at the wing roots and to the pilot control are "foolproof" and can be made when assembling in the field in a few moments. The wing is no more vulnerable to missiles than the ordinary fixed wing. Mention has already been made of this new achievement to Prof Hopkinson and at his suggestion I mention it here.

List of Patents taken out by John F Benton

9004/10	Kite Carrier
	Renewal Date:– April 1914
24945/10	Flying Stability and Speed
	Renewal Date:– October 1914
12375/11	Spring Wheels
	Renewal Date:– May 1915
12805/11	Collapsible Skids
	Renewal Date May 1915
10487/15	A wing, the ends of which can be washed out in camber and angle of attach while flying
	Renewal Date:– January 1916

RESERVE COPY.

N° 9004   A.D. 1910

Date of Application, 14th Apr., 1910
Complete Specification Left, 13th Oct., 1910—Accepted, 13th Apr., 1911

PROVISIONAL SPECIFICATION.

Improved Elevating and Returning Carrier for Kite or other Strings.

We, JOHN FREDERICK BENTON, Electrical Engineer, Ford Cottage, Pinkney's Green, Maidenhead, Berks, and WILLIAM ALLEN, Camera Maker, 31, York Road, Maidenhead, Berks, do hereby declare the nature of this invention to be as follows:—

5   The contrivance consists essentially of a banner flag or sail, so arranged as to be free to advance along a line under the pressure of the wind, carrying the object to be elevated with it in a clip.
        On arriving at a bobbin or stop fixed at any desired point on the aforesaid line, the banner is caused by impact to withdraw from the wind pressure, as by
10   rolling up like a roller spring blind or dropping clear from the body of the contrivance. The impact also causes the object elevated to be dropped if required.
        In the drawing, A A is a roller spring blind held transversely to the body B B. This body can be hooked to and slides along a kite- or other line K by means
15   of suitable clips C and D.
        In front of the roller spring blind shewn, is a spring clip E, the jaws of which grip the object to be elevated. This clip releases the object by striking against the bobbin placed as at F, and at the same time actuates the trigger shewn at G G G which releases the roller spring blind allowing it to roll up.
20   The carrier is now able to return under its own weight.
        Dated the 13th day of April, 1910.

                                          JOHN FREDERICK BENTON.
                                          WILLIAM ALLEN.

COMPLETE SPECIFICATION.

25   **Improved Elevating and Returning Carrier for Kite or other Strings.**

We, JOHN FREDERICK BENTON, Electrical Engineer, Ford Cottage, Pinkney's Green, Maidenhead, Berks, and WILLIAM ALLEN, Camera Maker, 31, York Road, Maidenhead, Berks, do hereby declare the nature of this invention and in what manner the same is to be performed, to be particularly described and ascertained
30   in and by the following statement:—

        This invention relates to improvements in apparatus of the kind in which an object held by a carrier is carried up a kite string by wind pressure on a sail attached to the carrier, the sail being released by the contact of the carrier with an obstruction on the string, whereupon the object is released if desired
35   and the sail is returned by a spring or the like to an inoperative position so that the carrier returns down the string by its own weight.
        In the drawing (left with our Provisional Specification) A A is a roller spring blind held transversely to the body B B.

A.D. 1910. April 14. N⁰ 9004.
BENTON & *another's* Provisional Specification.

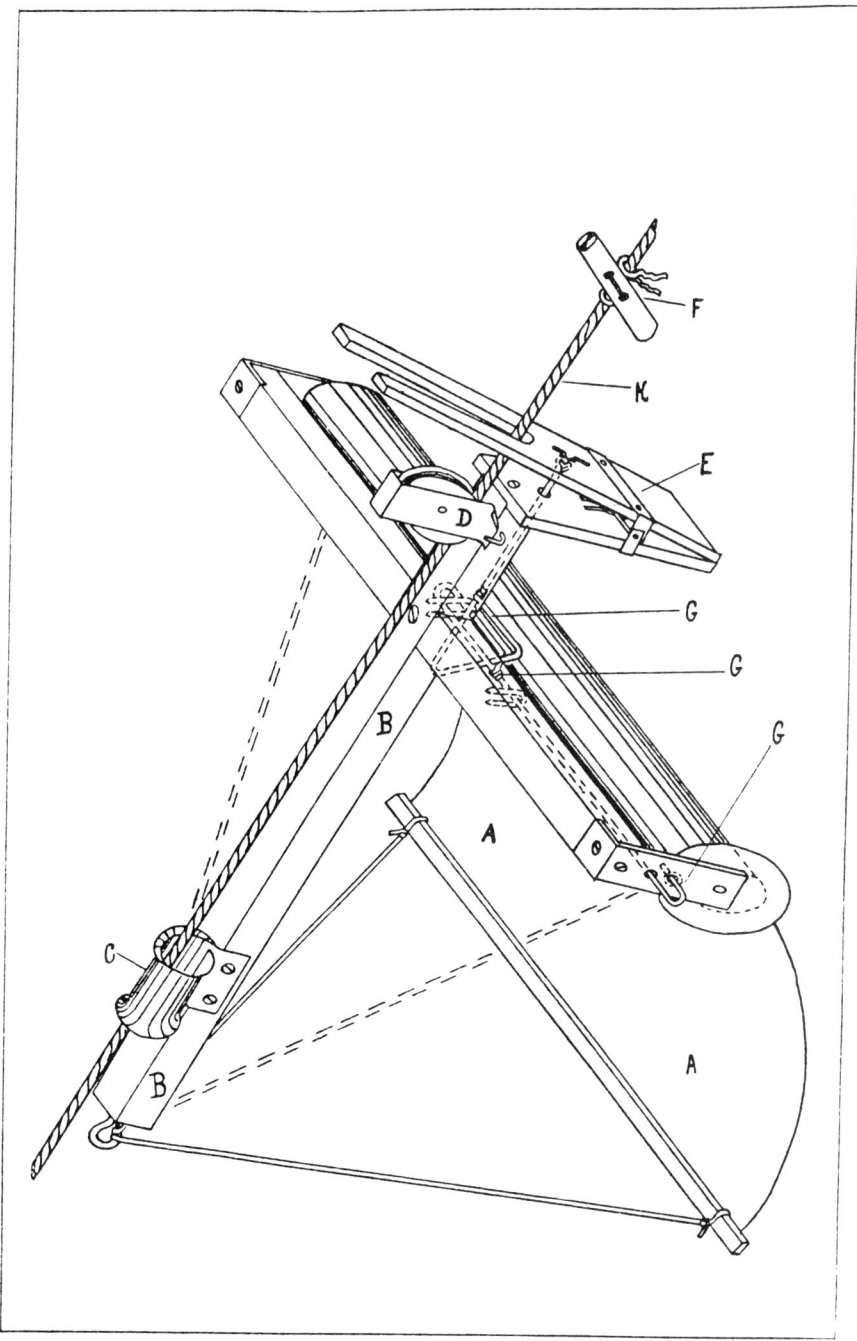

RESERVE COPY.

AMENDED SPECIFICATION.

Reprinted as amended under Section 8 of the Patents and Designs Act, 1907.

N° 24,945   A.D. 1910

Date of Application, 27th Oct., 1910
Complete Specification Left, 29th May, 1911—Accepted, 26th Oct., 1911

PROVISIONAL SPECIFICATION.

System for Longitudinal Balance of Flying Machines and Control of Flying Speed.

I, JOHN FREDERICK BENTON, Electrical Engineer, Ford Cottage, Pinkney's Green, Maidenhead, Berks, do hereby declare the nature of this invention to be as follows:—

The system applies to two or more surfaces, which may be monoplane, biplane, cellular or otherwise, placed in succession about the centre of gravity of the whole machine, and so arranged that, starting from the front of the machine, the angle of incidence of each succeeding surface, measured from the horizontal, increases.

These angles may be positive or negative as in Figure 1, in the accompanying drawing.

The values of the angles at which the surfaces are set, are directly dependent upon the longitudinal position of the centre of gravity of the machine, which may be any intermediate position.

Now, to meet conditions of the wind, such as gusts, to raise or lower the machine and to alter its speed of horizontal flight, the angles of some or of all the surfaces are altered, and stability is maintained by adhering to the above relation.

In the figure a machine is shewn diagrammatically with two biplanes A and B, with the centre of gravity at C and operated by a suitable differential gear at D, shewn separately at E. The differential gear being moved as a whole around the axis X Y, swings the back biplane B faster than the front A, either to positive or negative angular positions, that is, to angles above or below the horizontal H Z, and respectively decreases or increases the speed of flight, the whole time maintaining longitudinal stability; but if the machine is subjected to wind gusts or other alterations in the conditions of flight, or if the machine is required to rise or fall, the differential gear is then operated about the axis P Q, and the values of the angles of the (in this figure biplane-) surfaces relatively to one another, are slightly changed from their former simultaneous values, to maintain stability under the new conditions.

Dated the 26th day of October, 1910.

JOHN F. BENTON.

[Price 8d.]

PRICE 1/-
Price 5s. 0d.

System for Longitudinal Balance of Flying Machines and Control of Flying Speed.

COMPLETE SPECIFICATION (AMENDED).

System for Longitudinal Balance of Flying Machines and Control of Flying Speed.

I, JOHN FREDERICK BENTON, Electrical Engineer, Ford Cottage, Pinkney's Green, Maidenhead, Berks, do hereby declare the nature of this invention and in what manner the same is to be performed, to be particularly described and ascertained in and by the following statement:—

The longitudinal balance of flying machines depends upon the position of the centre of gravity, the area of the supporting surfaces, the position longitudinally of these surfaces, the sectional shape of the surfaces longitudinally the angles at which they are set from the horizontal and the position and disposition of the propelling force.

In order to vary the conditions of flight, some or all of these quantities must be varied and this invention consists in disposing the surfaces relatively to the centre of gravity in a definite way and in swinging the whole supporting surfaces by means of spiders as in the drawing left with my Provisional Specification about horizontal transverse axes so as to change their angles relatively to horizontal forward motion. The longitudinal section of the last or a part of the last of the supporting surfaces is also changeable as in the drawing filed herewith. It is preferable in a flying machine for convenience of housing and rigidity of structure that the width overall be not too great and that the weight be supported as equally as possible by the whole structure. I therefore arrange the two or more surfaces which are biplane cellular or otherwise in succession so that the centre of gravity of the whole machine lies between the supporting surfaces and is about 40% of the whole length measured from the leading edge of the first surface to the trailing edge of the last and of such areas that the resultant lifting moment of the supporting surfaces about the centre of gravity as fulcrum to the front shall equal that to the back, the chords of the longitudinal section of the supporting surfaces all being horizontal.

But in actual flight the succeeding surfaces move in air that has already been given a more or less downward trend by the reaction of the preceding surfaces and therefore their angles measured from the horizontal must be increased and the more so as the angles of the preceding surfaces increase. In this respect also provision must be made for the propelling force, for if propellers giving a horizontal thrust be placed in an intermediate longitudinal position they bring the deflected air stream more or less back to the horizontal due to their slipstream and the angles of the succeeding surfaces must be diminished correspondingly to maintain equilibrium. The position of the propellers above or below the centre of resistance to forward motion of the whole machine effects the angles of the supporting surfaces behind the propellers in a similar way.

It is obvious that the thrust from the propellers will within certain limits cause the machine to rise practically in proportion to the angles of incidence of the supporting surfaces and the rise and horizontal speed are therefore controlled by rotating the supporting surfaces simultaneously about their axes; the propeller thrust remaining the same, the smaller the angles the less will be the rise and the greater the horizontal speed and *vice versa*.

On the other hand if by uneven loading, wind gusts or other causes the conditions of equilibrium are changed then the ratio of the angles of the supporting surfaces in front of the centre of gravity to those behind it must be changed to restore equilibrium.

In the drawing filed herewith my machine is shewn with two biplanes A and B, swinging on spiders S S the hubs of which are situated nearly ⅓ the

System for Longitudinal Balance of Flying Machines and Control of Flying Speed.

width measured from the front or leading edge to the trailing edge of the planes and midway between them vertically. The centre of gravity is at C nearly 40% of the whole length measured from the leading edge of A to the trailing edge of B respectively. To the left side and in front of the aviator's
5 seat is a hand wheel which by rotating the worm W moves the system of levers K L M N O. The radius levers L and N are chosen of such lengths and the connecting rods K and O hinged to them at such intermediate points that the back biplane B is made to move nearly twice as fast as the front biplane A. The connecting rod M has a series of holes drilled at its ends to
10 enable the biplanes A and B to be initially set relatively to one another so as to give an even flying keel. Motion of the aforesaid hand-wheel rotating the worm W thus gives simultaneous alteration in the angles of incidence of both biplanes by rotating them on the spiders S S and the rise and therefore the speed of the machine is under direct control. If now the line of flight of the
15 machine is disturbed by a wind gust or if its equilibrium has been upset by unequal loading or other causes or if the machine is required to rise or descend on an oblique keel, then the centre of pressure on the whole machine is changed by moving the lever R placed at the aviator's right hand side which flexes the afterpart of the top central portion of the back biplane B by means of the
20 cables T T and so by changing its longitudinal sectional shape the lift of the back biplane is decreased or increased and equilibrium restored thereby or the required inclination given to the machine. I am aware that in a biplane machine it has been proposed to provide a pair of supplementary elevating planes connected together in the form of a biplane by means of an X-frame.
25 In my invention the vertical steering is effected solely by the hinged portion of the back main plane, and my spider-supported planes serve entirely as main lifting planes.

Having now particularly described and ascertained the nature of my said invention, and in what manner the same is to be performed, I declare that what
30 I claim is:

1. In a flying machine the disposition of succeeding moveable spiderborn supporting biplane surfaces so that the centre of gravity is situated nearly 40% of the distance measured from the leading edge of the first biplane to the trailing edge of the last respectively, for the purpose set forth.

35 2. The manner of supporting lifting biplane surfaces on spiders each arranged in one plane or substantially in one plane, and capable of rotating about an axis, vertically midway between the surfaces and horizontally about ⅓ the distance measured from the front or leading edge to the trailing edge of the biplane respectively.

40 3. A flying machine composed of two spiderborn supporting biplane surfaces capable of rotation about a transverse axis and operated by a system of levers coupled to one common worm in conjunction with a hinged portion of the back of the last or part of the last biplane surface substantially as set forth and described herein.

45 Dated the 4th day of September, 1911.

JOHN FREDERICK BENTON.

Redhill: Printed for His Majesty's Stationery Office, by Love & Malcomson, Ltd.—1912.

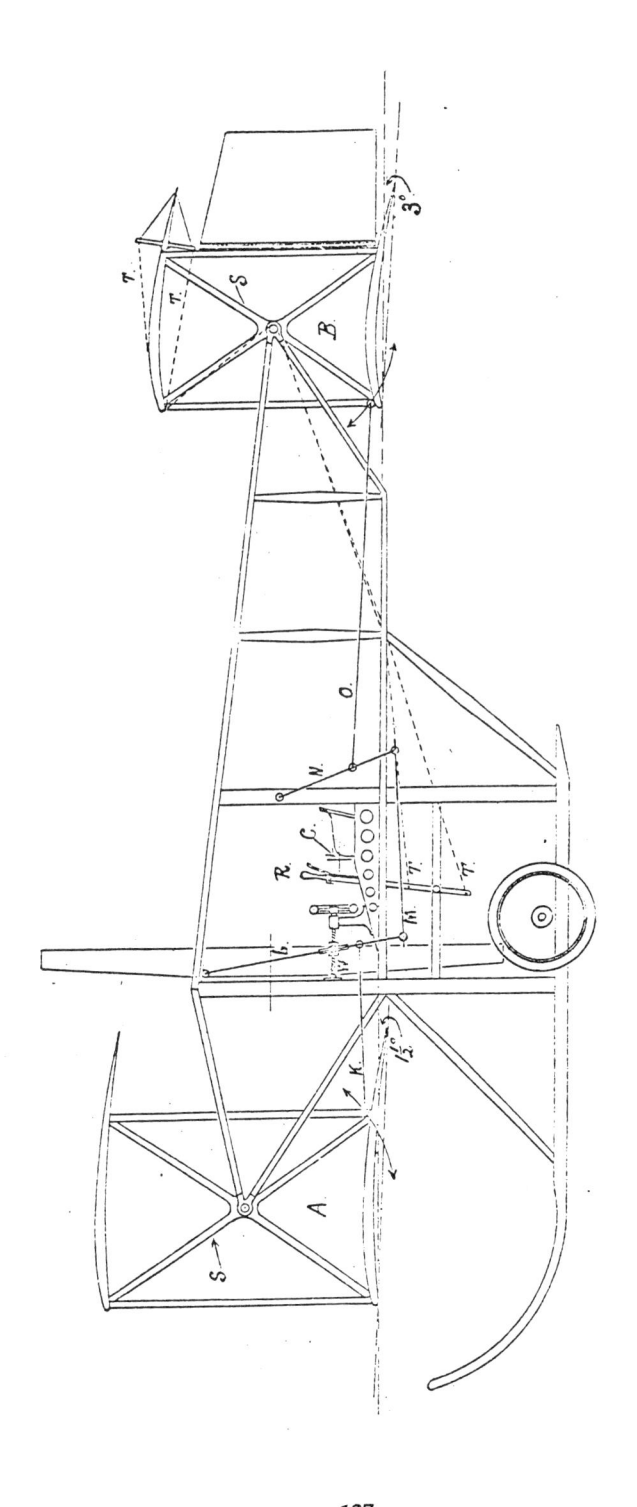

This drawing is a reproduction of the original on a reduced scale

This drawing is a reproduction of the original on a reduced scale

N° 12,375　A.D. 1911

Date of Application, 23rd May, 1911
Complete Specification Left, 23rd Nov., 1911—Accepted, 7th Mar., 1912

PROVISIONAL SPECIFICATION.

Spring System for Supporting Flying Machines Resiliently on Wheels.

I, JOHN FREDERICK BENTON, Electrical Engineer, Ford Cottage, Pinkneys Green, Maidenhead, Berks, do hereby declare the nature of this invention to be as follows:—

5　The system consists of a pair of wheels mounted on one axle, which is transverse to and above the skid or other longitudinal member of a flying machine, and is held in place by two pairs of tension springs, one end of each of the pairs being attached to lugs fixed on the axle between the wheels and near to the wheel hubs.

The other ends of the springs are fixed one from each side of the axle towards the front and one from each side to the back of the skid (or other longitudinal
10　flying machine member) by suitable plates and bolts, the four springs thus forming a diamond shaped figure as viewed in plan and of which the wheel axle is one diagonal and the skid the other.

The springs are given a tension suitable for the load to be supported and may be of rubber, metal or other suitable material.

15　The device in its above simplest form is suitable for a double skidded machine, like most biplanes, but in machines such as monoplanes in which there is generally only one skid below the machine, additional tension springs are attached from the sides of the machine to the aforesaid axle lugs to prevent the machine completely heeling over about the skid.

20　Dated the 22nd day of May, 1911.

JOHN F. BENTON.

COMPLETE SPECIFICATION.

Spring System for Supporting Flying Machines Resiliently on Wheels.

I, JOHN FREDERICK BENTON, Electrical Engineer, Ford Cottage, Pinkneys
25　Green, Maidenhead, Berks, do hereby declare the nature of this invention and in what manner the same is to be performed, to be particularly described and ascertained in and by the following statement:—

The system consists of a pair of wheels mounted on one axle which is transverse to and above the skid or other longitudinal member of a flying machine
30　and which is held in place by two pairs of tension springs, one end of each of the pairs being attached to lugs fixed on the axle between the wheels and near to the wheel hubs.

The other ends of the springs are fixed one from each side of the axle towards the front and one from each side of the back of the skid (or other longitudinal
35　flying machine member) by suitable plates and bolts, the four springs thus forming a diamond shaped figure as viewed in plan and of which the wheel axle is one diagonal and the skid the other. The springs are given a suitable

[*Price 8d.*]

Spring System for Supporting Flying Machines Resiliently on Wheels.

tension for the load to be supported and may be of rubber metal or other suitable material.

In the accompanying drawing S S and S¹ S¹ are the two pairs of tension springs attached to the wheel axle near the hubs at L L and to the skid C by suitable screweyes at A and B. The weight of the machine is transmitted down 5 the stanchions P to the skid and then through the springs to the axle but close to the wheel hubs the tendency of the axle to bend in the middle is reduced to a minimum and this system does away with side springs, bobbins and radius rods and cables since it gives to any combination of side and upward strain.

Having now particularly described and ascertained the nature of my said 10 invention and in what manner the same is to be performed I declare that what I claim is:—

A combination of springs forming a lozenge attached in part to the wheel axle near the hubs of the wheels, and in part to a bottom longitudinal member of a flying machine. 15

Dated the 23rd day of November, 1911.

JOHN FREDERICK BENTON.

Redhill: Printed for His Majesty's Stationery Office, by Love & Malcomson, Ltd.—1912.

A.D. 1911. May 23. N⁰ 12,375.
BENTON'S Complete Specification.

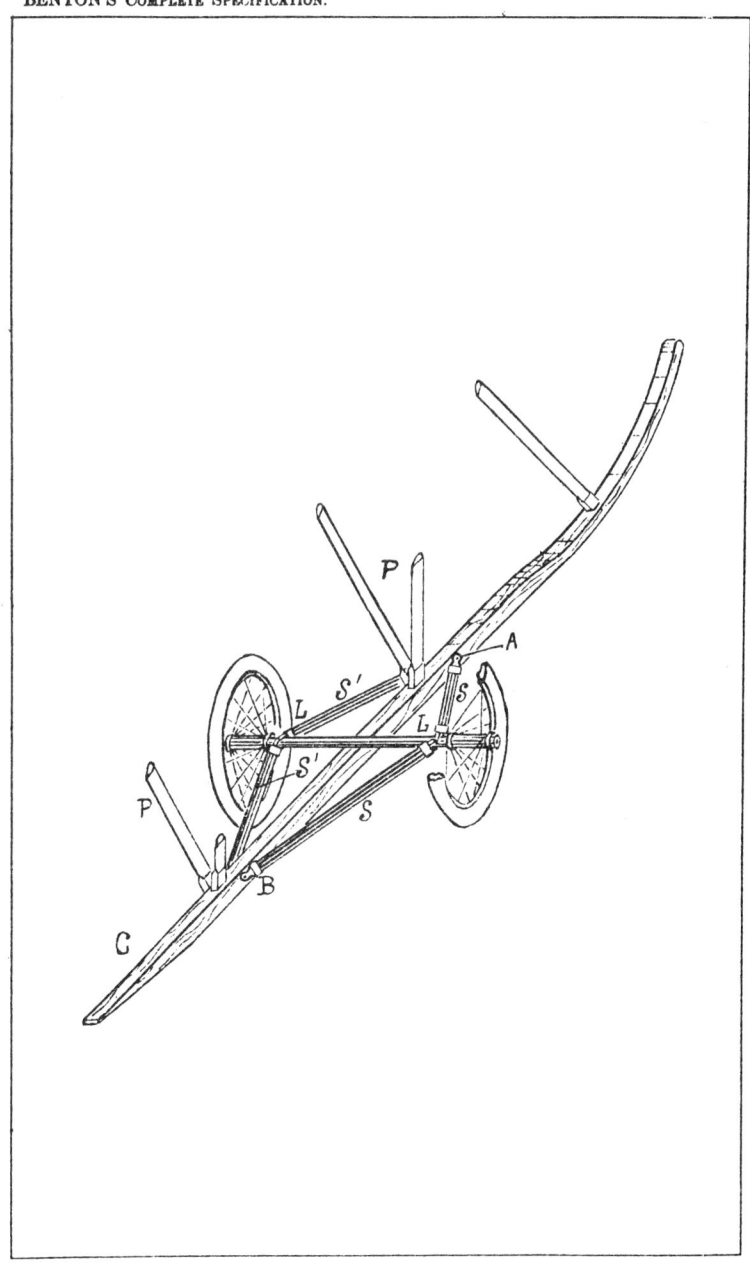

A.D. 1911. May 29 N° 12,805.
BENTON'S Complete Specification.

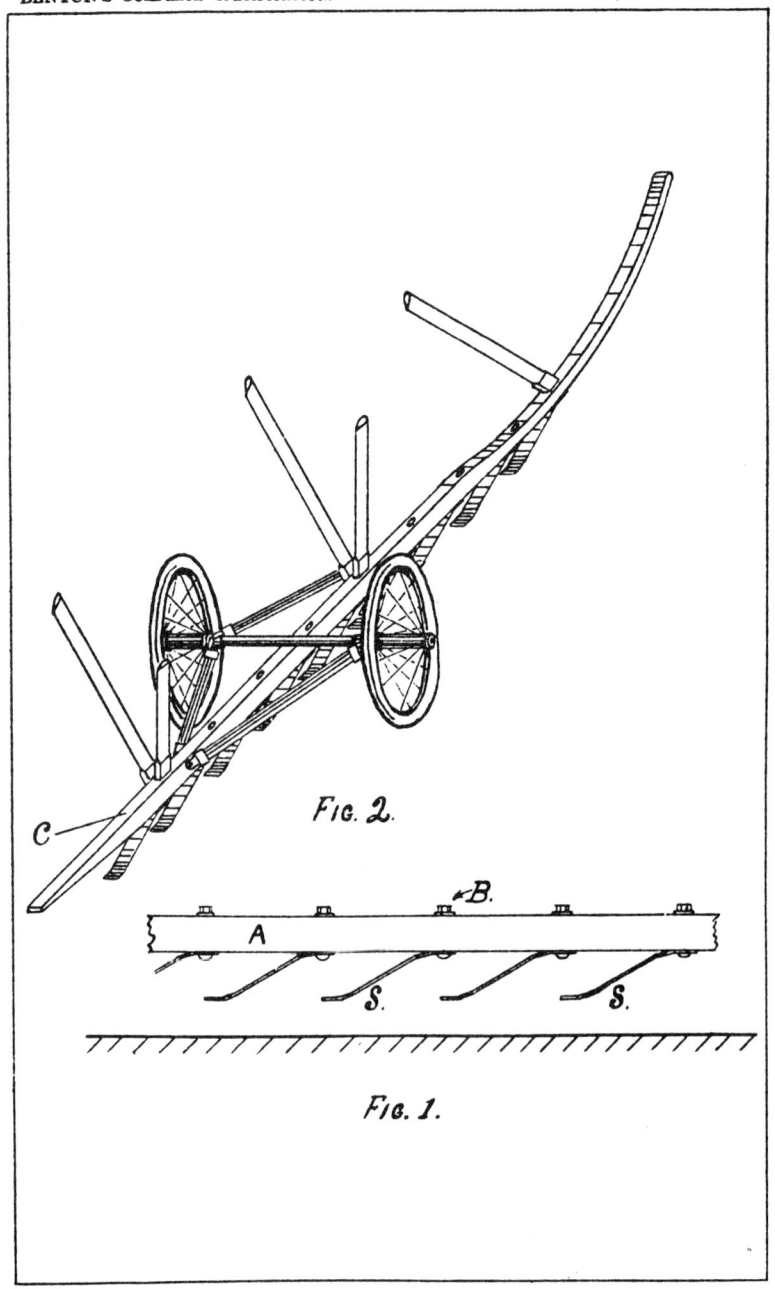

Fig. 2.

C

Fig. 1.

A B S S

N° 12,805　　A.D. 1911

Date of Application, 29th May, 1911
Complete Specification Left, 29th Nov., 1911—Accepted, 7th Mar., 1912

PROVISIONAL SPECIFICATION.

Collapsible Spring Skids for Flying Machines.

I, JOHN FREDERICK BENTON, Electrical Engineer, Ford Cottage, Pinkneys Green, Maidenhead, Berks., do hereby declare the nature of this invention to be as follows:—

The invention consists of two bars one above the other and parallel for the
5 working portion of their length; the lower bar is the skid, the upper bar a suitable longitudinal member of the flying machine or a parallel portion of the body of the machine. These two parts can approach each other under shock, against the resistance of springs placed between them.

To an extent the construction is dependent upon the amount of collapse allow-
10 able and on the shape of the under chassis of the machine.

If only slight collapse is required the lower bar or skid is distanced from the aforesaid upper bar or suitable longitudinal member of the flying machine by flat steel springs as used on coster barrows bolted between them and slanting from front to back of the machine downwards.

15 If securely bolted these tend to resist side displacement of the skid but are resilient to vertical and longitudinal shock. Or they can be bolted so as to swivel and will then also take side shock, as when at landing, the flying machine is carried bodily sideways by a side wind.

Dated the 27th day of May, 1911.
20　　　　　　　　　　　　　　　　　　　　　　JOHN F. BENTON.

COMPLETE SPECIFICATION.

Collapsible Spring Skids for Flying Machines.

I, JOHN FREDERICK BENTON, Electrical Engineer, Ford Cottage, Pinkney's Green, Maidenhead, Berks., do hereby declare the nature of this invention
25 and in what manner the same is to be performed, to be particularly described and ascertained in and by the following statement:—

The invention consists in applying springs in a particular way to a bottom longitudinal member such as a skid or skids of a flying machine and in such a manner as to absorb the shock of landing and to allow such skids to travel side-
30 ways over the ground without ricking over and breaking the chassis as in a bad landing sideways or over rough ground. The device comprises a number of flat strip springs made of steel, hard duralumin or other elastic material slanting from front to back downwards and shaped in such a manner as to form a running surface some distance below the aforesaid skids to which they are bolted on the
35 underside so that they can turn freely and constitute a number of small spring skids trailing in the direction of travel of the machine at the time.

In my accompanying drawing in Figure 1. S S are the shaped flat springs bolted in succession to a bottom longitudinal portion A of a flying machine by

N° 12,805.—A.D. 1911.

Collapsible Spring Skids for Flying Machines.

means of the bolts B, about which they can turn and accomodate themselves to any direction of motion below the portion A. Figure 2. shews my invention applied to a flying machine skid C, indicating the natural position relative to wheels *etc.* of the aforesaid shaped flat springs.

Having now particularly described and ascertained the nature of my said invention and in what manner the same is to be performed, I declare that what I claim is :—

A series of shaped flat springs attached to the underpart of a flying machine skid and capable of rotating about the holding on bolts to accomodate themselves to the line of motion of the flying machine over the ground and give resiliently to shock.

Dated the 29th day of November, 1911.

JOHN F. BENTON.

Redhill: Printed for His Majesty's Stationery Office, by Love & Malcomson, Ltd.—1912.

Provisional Patent

No 10487/15

John F Benton

July 1915

  Means of varying the effective lifting surface of flying machines and of balancing the opposing wing tip resistances when turning and banking. The invention consists essentially of a rocker from the ends of which cables freely pass, controlling surfaces that form a part of the wing tips of a flying machine. The other ends of these cables leave the rocker arm near its axis of rotation and are there joined together and fastened to a worm or suitable lever so arranged that the cables may be simultaneously tightened or slackened by moving this worm or lever.

1. On slackening the cables the effective lifting area at the wing tips is decreased since the trailing portion controlled by these cables and which may be hinged or flexible, is flattened out and brought more and more into such a position that the air is no longer accelerated downwards by the forward motion of the wing. To assist this movement of the trailing portion of the wing, suitable springs (as of rubber) are attached on the topside thereof. Conversely on tightening the cables the wing is brought back to its normal condition or may be flexed beyond this point.
2. On the other hand the rocker can be partly rotated or rocked by cables from the control or steering column, conveniently operating over a quadrant fixed to the rocker, and in this way a differential motion is given to the wing ends of the aforesaid wing control cables for lateral balance of the flying machine as in the ordinary way. The above motions do not interfere with one another so that the wing tips can be flattened out or restored for variation of speed simultaneously with their differential movement for lateral balance.
3. The ends of the rocker from which the cables pass to wing tips are bent back out of line and the cables after leaving these ends are crossed and then pass over pulleys or through runners so situate that when the rocker is partly rotated or rocked, whereas the cable from one is very much slackened that from the other moves nearly about the geometrical dead centre and is therefore tightened but little.

  Conversely after being brought back to the normal transverse position and then rocked to the other side the conditions of the cables' motions are reversed. These cables are fastened to the underneath side of the flexing wing tips so that the movements of the wing tips correspond with the aforesaid motions of these cables. For banking or turning, as to the pilot's right hand side, the wing tip on the pilot's left hand side is given a very slightly increased lifting position in which its resistance to forward motion of the flying machine is but slightly increased but the wing tip on the pilot's right side is moved into a considerably decreased lifting position in which its resistance to forward motion of the flying machine is increased above that of the other side and the aerodynamic forces are in this way balanced for stable banking and turning. The proper adjustment of the forces is brought about by the mechanical proportions of the device.

Drawing of Benton Wing, Patent No. 10487/15

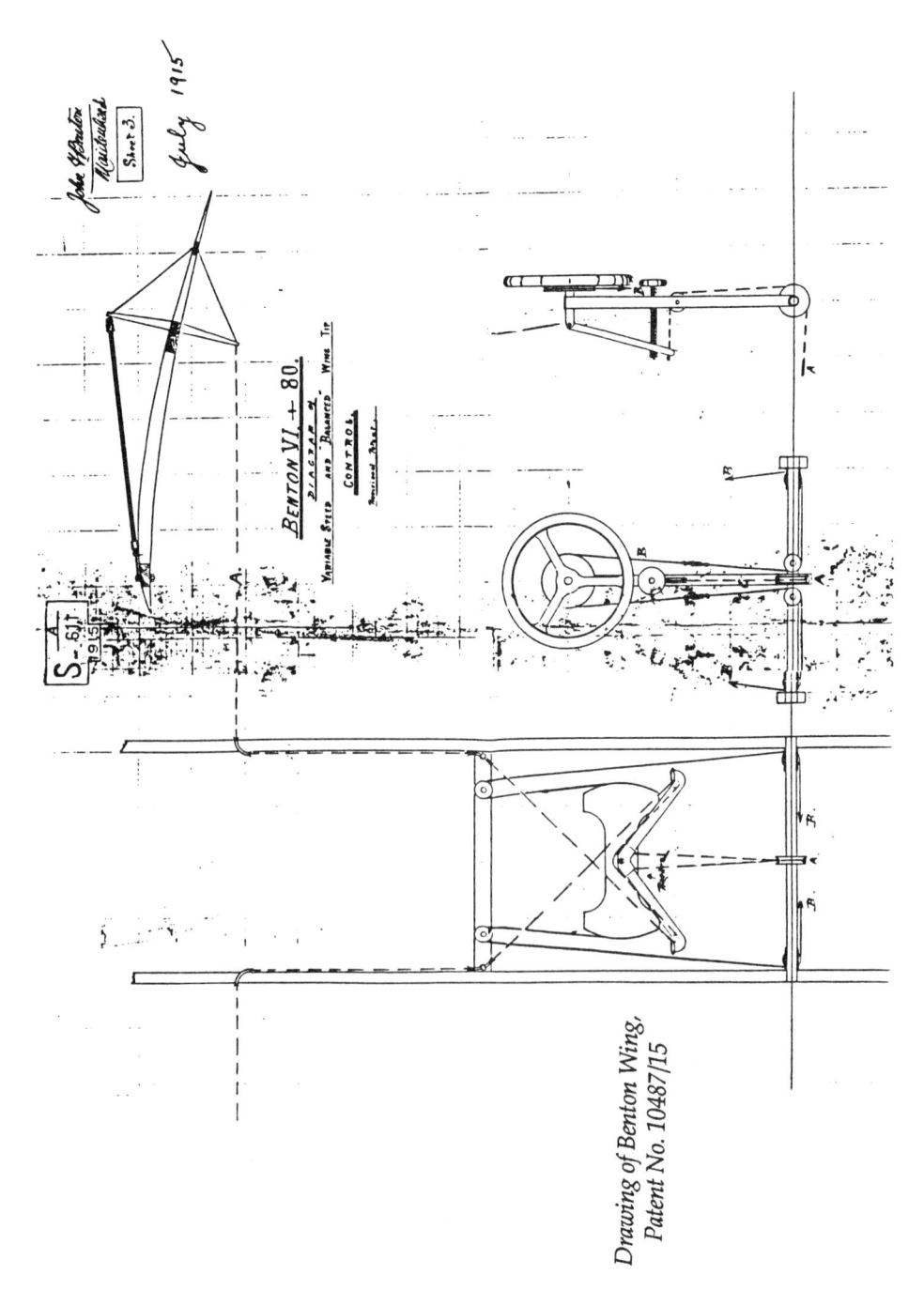

Form P. App. 5.

Any further communication on this subject should be addressed to:—
THE COMPTROLLER,
THE PATENT OFFICE,
25, SOUTHAMPTON BUILDINGS,
LONDON, W.C.
(*Telegraphic Address*:—PATENT OFFICE, LONDON.)
(*Telephone No.*:—5301 CITY.)
and the following number should be quoted in the communication:—

10487/15

THE PATENT OFFICE,

25, SOUTHAMPTON BUILDINGS,

LONDON, W.C.

27 JUL 1915

Sir,

    With reference to your application for a patent, numbered as above, the Examiner has reported that the title does not sufficiently indicate the subject matter of the invention described in your specification; and I have therefore, in accordance with section 3, sub-section (2), of the Patents and Designs Act, 1907, to request that, as regards the title, you will be good enough to amend the documents returned herewith. Any title submitted by you will be duly considered. (See note VII. over.)

    The following title would appear to indicate the subject matter of the invention, and would be accepted if substituted for the present title on forms 1 and 2, viz:- "Improvements in or relating to aeroplanes".

    The description is not clear. If you could furnish a rough sketch of your invention, this would probably facilitate examination; but the sketch should not be referred to in the specification.

    In view of the present state of War and of recent Royal Proclamations, and in view also of the Patents, Designs and Trade Marks (Temporary Rules) Acts, 1914, I have to ask you, in accordance with the settled prac-
-tice, to be good enough to fill in column 2 of the accompanying form, to sign the declaration at the foot thereof, and to return the same to this Office.

    The application form, provisional specification and a Declaration Form are enclosed.

        I am, Sir,

        Your obedient Servant,

Arthur Reeves

For the manner of amending documents
see the notes at the back of this sheet.

J.F.Beaton, Esq.
  Ford House,
    Pinkney's Green,
      Maidenhead,
        Berks.

(58,651). Wt.8245—3266. 4000. 6/12. A.&E.W.
(74,690) „ 45,623—3490. 5000. 3/13.

```
Any further communication on this subject
should be addressed to :—
        THE COMPTROLLER.
          THE PATENT OFFICE.
          25, SOUTHAMPTON BUILDINGS,
                    LONDON, W.C.
  (Telegraphic Address.—PATENT OFFICE, LONDON.)
  (Telephone No.:—3301 CITY.)
and the following number should be quoted in
the communication :—
            10487/15.
```

THE PATENT OFFICE.

25, SOUTHAMPTON BUILDINGS,

LONDON, W.C.

14 AUG.

Sir,

With reference to your application, numbered as above, and in reply to your letter of the 30th ultimo, the Examiner reports that the description may commence in the way you suggest.

In the sketch that you have filed, there appears to be too many ends to the cords. The pencil sketch below the main figure appears to him to be the full path of the cord but that does not appear to quite to agree with the description. You should make clear the correct path of the cord in the description and return the sketch with the amended documents.

The provisional specification and sketch are enclosed. *sketch is*

I am, Sir,

Your obedient Servant,

The words "and through" added in 2nd line of — description

J.F.Benton, Esq.,
    Ford House,
        Pinkney's Green,
            Maidenhead,
                Berks.

For the manner of amending documents, see the notes at the back of this sheet.

Any further communication on this subject should be addressed to :—
THE COMPTROLLER,
THE PATENT OFFICE,
25, SOUTHAMPTON BUILDINGS,
LONDON, W.C.
(*Telegraphic Address* :—PATENT OFFICE, LONDON.)
(*Telephone No.* :—5591 CITY.)
and the following number should be quoted in the communication :—

10487/15

THE PATENT OFFICE,

25, SOUTHAMPTON BUILDINGS,

LONDON, W.C.

21 AUG 1915

Sir,

    With reference to your application, numbered as above, the Examiner reports that the path of the cables B is still not clear on the sketch. The description must be made clear without reference to the sketch as this will not form part of the specification.

    Page 1 of the specification should be rewritten on the enclosed blank copy of form 2.

    The provisional specification and sketch are also enclosed.

              I am, Sir,

                  Your obedient Servant,

Sect Pat. Nov 27/15

J.F. Beaton, Esq.
    Ford House,
        Pinkney's Green,
             Maidenhead.

For the manner of amending documents, see the notes at the back of this sheet.

Patent No 10487/15, the Benton Wing, was never completed and was subsequently abandoned.

There follows a series of letters which Johnny wrote to various people appealing for help to get his aeroplane design accepted, they include a report he wrote on the whole exercise.

This letter, written to a friend, tells of Johnny's decision to join the Army brought on by his failure to interest the authorities in his aeroplanes and his ideas.

My Dear Knowles   13th March 1915

It is a deuce of a time since I have heard or seen anything of you so I hope you are still in the land of the living. I had not forgotten that I was to meet you in Town some time but owing to stress of work I have not yet been able to manage it. Personally I have not yet joined up in the army although I have attested and have been put back, but what will ultimately transpire I do not know as I am particularly interested in a new type of aeroplane invented by a friend of mine and have helped in its construction. He is in negotiation with the Government and should it be taken up I shall be required to help supervise. Now I am spending the weekend with him and he tells me that there is a matter of urgency with regard to some of his patents and he is in doubt as to how to proceed.

I shall therefore be grateful if you can arrange a meeting with us, as any action which has to be taken must be taken before next Monday.

                              John F Benton

G L E W

                               Bray Road

                              Maidenhead

                             19th June 1915

Dear Mr Stringer

Many thanks for your letter which reached me last evening and for the trouble you are taking. As you have seen the machine, I think it will be best to give brief details and points in this letter:

1. Patented device for varying the effective wing area giving variable speeds while flying and for minimising loss of altitude when turning.
2. Arranging decreasing liability to dive through mistakes in control.
3. Special design against nose dives (in part experimentally evolved).
4. Extremely low head resistance of design.

5. High efficiency wing curve arrived at by actual calculation.
6. High efficiency propellor.
7. Low weight (910) lbs. For exceedingly robust design.
8. Resulting from nos 5 to 7, high speed for comparative small hp ranging from about 35 to 50 mph in the air with a 35 – 40 hp N E C 2 stroke, water cooled engine, weight about 223 lbs.
10. Patented flexible wheel system of unlimited life which makes the machine extremely flexible on the ground so that I have been able to carry out all my experiments with these machines in very small meadows, and can come down in very confined spaces. Can turn machine in its own length at about 20 mph.
11. All parts are standardised and interchangeable where necessary.
12. The whole chassis, which is most likely to be damaged, can be removed from under the fuselage and a new one replaced as one unit.

John F Benton
2nd Lieut H L Stringer, R E
Wireless W T Station, Slough
at Chalvey

Sequence of Correspondence with Admiralty, Whitehall 1915

July 2nd	I write Sec Admiralty – seven years flying etc.
July 12th	I write further to above and ask for early reply and that B 6 has been mentioned at Admiralty by Chalvey Wireless (Stringer).
July 12th	I write Lord Fisher, B 6 at Chalvey, will he help to bring to official notice.
July 23rd	B of I and R write me 12th inst – same has been sent to Admiralty.
July 26th	Air Dept Admiralty re 2nd inst has been passed onto Director of Air Department, Admiralty and wants drawings B 6 and details.
Aug 4th	I send drawings to Director of Air Dept, Admiralty with descriptive spec etc and want to shew machine to them in reply to theirs of 26th inst (AI 25780/4096).
Aug 6th	B of I acknowledge letter of 12th July, and have it sent on to Admiralty.
Aug 7th	Admiralty acknowledge my letter of 12th July.
Aug 12th	I write Admiralty, Director Air Department, am again sending roll of drawings etc, which had been returned by Admiralty in error to me.
Sept 3rd	I write Admiralty, Air Department, saying what speed I anticipate with 100 hp engine.
Sept 4th	I write Mr Harris–Booth at Admiralty re B 6 and seven years and 100 mph speed, we could not see him at Admiralty when we called last (corridors) week.
Sept 4th	B of Inv acknowledged receipt of my letter July 12th, to say my suggestions have been investigated and are of no practical utility.
Sept 16th	B of Inv ask for brief description of proposals and enclose "confidential" circular. But before I reply comes next letter.
Sept 23rd	B of Inv reply to my letter of 4th inst to Commander Bridge but that my proposals add nothing to the information already in their possession.
Sept 25th	I write B of Inv in reply to their refusal I would like interview, sure of a misapprehension.
Sept 29th	B of Inv reply no use for interview and that "purchase and supply" concerns Director of Air Services, Admiralty!

Oct 19th	Admiralty Air Department, reply to my letter of Sept 3rd, don't want this type of machine!
Nov 30th	I ask Sec of Admiralty to return my two sets of drawings and descriptive matter.
Dec 3rd	Sec of Admiralty returns one set only and yet says no record is now kept at Admiralty!

NOTE: On 4th September JFB went to the Admiralty building to see a Mr Harris–Booth, sadly he got lost and failed to keep his appointment – the word "CORRIDORS" in brackets refers to this mishap!

Record of letters with Admiralty through Stringer 1915

June 18th	Lt Stringer writes me to say he has not yet heard from Admiralty Air Department.
June 19th	I send particulars B 6 which he has seen at hangar.
June 25th	Stringer offers to do his best at War Office or Admiralty.
June 28th	Stringer writes to say reply at last from Admiralty and encloses letters from Mr Garton.
June 30th	I return letters from Mr Garton and write Stringer.
July 14th	Stringer sends me Admiralty letter dated July 12th 1915 SA 553/15/502.
July 19th	I write Sec of Admiralty in reply.
Aug 13th	Telegram from Admiralty – saying come to Chalvey in afternoon August 13th 1915.
Aug 13th	I show machine. Reps express appreciation of machine.
Aug 22nd	Stringer sends me Admiralty letter dated Aug 19th, SA 611/15/601, refusing my machine, no reason given.
Sept 3rd	I write Sec of Admiralty re speed of machine with 100 hp engine and can we get interview to clear up any possible misapprehension because reps approved of machine. No reply.
	We interview sub–editor of Daily Express and sends us on to editor of "Aeroplane" Mr Grey. Grey warns us in conversation and advises us to try some firm, eg Vickers, Major Wood.
Oct 8th	Grey writes RAF are trying my wings but use plus pull, therefore fail.
Oct 12th	I tell him why they have failed, I let the ailerons up.
Oct 13th	Grey acknowledges my letter and is giving the RAF people this further information.
Nov 15th	We see Captain Acland at Vickers but left no drawings.
Nov 22nd	We write Grey that had called but he was busy. Tell him of new B 7 wing and of our interview with Hopkinson re our treatment and want an agreement. Also that we had seen Captain Acland and had shown him B 7 drawings, and that Captain Acland said that Vickers experienced same difficulties.

Nov 24th	Grey acknowledges letter and says we shall be liable to same treatment that other people have to suffer if RAF get it. Most important statement. Better go to some honourable business firm, I certainly think highly of your B 7.
Nov 26th	I send blue–prints of B 6 and description to Vickers secretary.
Dec 4th	Vickers wants B 7 information.
Dec 10th	We see Major Wood at Vickers and elaborate verbally B 6 control, chassis and wheels and talked over question of disclosure of B 7 explaining that Government had it subjudicae. He offers to build machine to our design.
Dec 14th	They want me to go to Crayford to shew Flanders our B 7.
Dec 16th	I reply that I cannot go to Crayford at present and therefore the matter is subjudicae with Admiralty and another step has been made by them.

2nd Lieut H L Stringer, R E
Wireless W T Station
Chalvey, Slough

List of Organisations contacted by John F Benton

Admiralty Board of Inventions and Research

Professor B Hopkinson, Floor 3, Victory House, S W

War Office Board of Inventions

Major General Hickman

Air Department, Captain Cook

Air Finance Department, Mr A Turner

E Russell-Clarke, Esq, Room 406 b, Admiralty, (II Kings Bench Walk, Temple, E C)

Vickers Marine Ltd, Broadway, Westminster

Major Wood and Captain Acland (Aviation Department)

Russian Embassy, Chesham House, Chesham Place, S W

    1. Military Attache General Yeruieloff, 3 Whitehall Court, S W

    2. Assistant Miltary Attache, Colonel Nicolieff

    3. Engineer's Department, Captain Mironoff, India House, Kingsway, W C

P T B Commission Francaise d'aclat a Londres

Aeronautique et Genie, M le Capitaine Plaisant, Canada House, Kingsway, W C

Military Attache, French Embassy, Albert Gate, S W

Military Attache, Italian Embassy, 20 Grosvenor Square, Park Lane, W

Military Attache, Japanese Embasy, 10 Grosvenor Square, Park Lane, W

Mr Grey, Editor of "Aeroplane", 166 Piccadilly

R C Lyle, Daily Express, St Brides Street, E C

Lt H C Stringer, Chalvey Wireless Station, Woodside Marlow, Egham House, Bourne End, Bucks

9th November 1915

A particularly significant private letter to John F Benton from an officer in the R F C who saw the B 6 at Chalvey

R F C Mess 12th August 1915
Farnborough

Dear Mr Benton

I received the drawings this morning and have forwarded them to the proper authorities.

I don't know whether you care to have my opinion of that matter, but treating this as a private letter, I think I ought to tell you that there is very little chance of the R F C buying your machine.

However I am certain you could get a position either as an equipment officer or in the factory here on the inspection department if you feel so disposed to serve your country.

Anyway this is just by the way and nothing to do with me at all.

Yours sincerely

A F A Hooper

BRAY ROAD,   October 7th 1915
MAIDENHEAD.   No 14

W. ALLEN

MANUFACTUER OF
High-Class Cameras,
- - Dark Slides, - -
STANDS, &c.

Lenses, Fittings &c.   TERMS. Cash with Order.

G. Russell Clarke Esq.
Pixley Wireless Matters.

Dear Mr. Clarke,

Enclosed herewith you will find brief statement of points of my Biplane which I had the pleasure and good fortune to show you yesterday.

Believe me, I am most grateful for your trouble and kind effort, coming as it does at a time when I had almost given up hope of placing the machine with the War Office or Admiralty.

Yours very sincerely,
John H. Benton

To G Russell–Clarke, Esq
Chalvey Wireless Station

Benton Aeroplanes
G L E W
7th October 1915

Benton VI plus 100 hp
Variable Speed Tractor Biplane

1. Special control for varying the effective wing area, by washing out the wing tips.
2. And minimising loss of altitude when turning. The inner and slower moving wing having the greater resistance.
3. Flexible wheel system of unlimited life. This takes up every kind of landing and travelling shock.
4. This system together with steerable tail skid controlled by cables separate from rudder cables has enabled me to carry out all my experiments from confined meadows and on rough ground.
5. The entire chassis can be removed from under the machine and replaced as one unit. Weight 100 lbs.
6. Stanchions and wing spars are universally hinged, therefore quick assemblage without constraint being set up.
7. All parts are standardised and interchangeable where necessary.
8. The body up to engine section is entirely built up of 3 ply on four longerons. The lines are good, ending without discontinuity in the wire edge of the tail planes.
9. Low head resistance of design; high efficiency wing curve and propellor, arrived at by calculation; special design against nose dives.
10. Machine is very robust and weight is low, 1230 lbs including 550 lbs, water–cooled 100 hp engine.
11. Maximum speed with wing tings fully washed out, above 100 mph.
12. Range of speed with 35 hp N E C is 33 to 52 mph.

Green Lane Engineering Works
Bray Road
Maidenhead, Berkshire
Flying Grounds: Chalvey near Slough

Mr G Russell–Clarke W Allen's Camera Works
Chief Engineer Maidenhead
Chalvey Wireless Station 2nd Nov 1915
Slough, Bucks

Dear Mr Russell–Clarke

Many thanks indeed for your letter enclosing Mr Hopkinson's which I return herewith. I have prepared a new set of drawings for him together with the descriptive matter he requires and have written to ask when he can see me. I have also written to attempt to recover drawings and specifications already sent and thank you for the advice.

Now I have some really good news for you, perhaps you will call to mind when we were returning from the hangar discussing the mechanical possibility of altering the actual wing area exposed during flight, that I thought it was not impossible. I was on the verge of accomplishing this and I have now done so. I am now able during flight to alter three dimensions of the wings at the same time. The total extra load involved in a 43 ft span machine is about 65 lbs inclusive, over my present weight. I retain my present system and add to it change of span (area) and chord. My range of speed and rate of ascent are greatly enhanced. May I have your indulgence so far as to ask you to let me know at your early convenience how I am to approach Mr Hopkinson on this matter, as I am not this time prepared to show any drawings or models of the new wings until I have some form of agreement from "the Powers that be". Assuring you that I am using every bit of ingenuity that I may possess to produce for the country a machine particularly wanted at this time, and thanking you in anticipation of your continued interest.

I am,
Yours very sincerely,
John F Benton

Sir Henry Dalziel, MP 23rd February 1916
Mr H Jaynson–Hicks, MP

Dear Sir

During the last eight years I have been engaged on aeronautical experiments in relation to aeroplanes and I have built six machines in all embodying the principles which have proved satisfactory in the previous ones, and to show that my machines have proved eminently practical I may state that being contemporary with the beginning of the movement my sole experience in actual flying has necessarily been gained with my own machines. Since the outbreak of war I have approached the War Office with a view to adopting my latest model which is considerably faster than existing machines mainly owing to a new type of wing which I have introduced. The reason I am writing you is that the question is essentially one of public interest, for the War Office sent down representatives to see the machine over which they waxed enthusiastic and requested drawings, which were covered by patents. In the outcome I ultimately received notification that they did not wish to consider the matter further but they did not return the drawings. Later we heard through outside sources that the aircraft factory were experimenting on their own account by means of the information I had supplied. This was about six months ago and now we hear that the government have placed orders with various firms for the supply of wings of our model to be fitted to existing machines which proves the worth of the invention. Now unfortunately this is not the end of the experience. Since the machine was first brought to the notice of the Army in the course of my continued researches by means of further inventions, I have again improved the efficiency of the machines and on the advice of a newspaper editor who warned me that what did actually happen would happen, I applied to Vickers who offered to take up the invention, but before accepting their offer I put that the Government should have a further opportunity of taking up this latest invention and as the Admiralty were reputed to the straightforward in their dealings I approached them. Now in spite of the fact that Vickers made their offer, the Admiralty after consultation by the aeroplane Sub-committee refuse either to take it up or to undertake experiments on the lines indicated which has been in the past, as I have mentioned, the fore-runner of quasi independent investigations on their own account. It will I think be obvious to you that such a backhanded procedure robbing the inventor of the fruits of his research is subversive of the true interests of the country, as when the matter gets known unless the practice is stopped no inventor will give the Government the opportunity of taking up or even investigating the possibilities of his invention. I shall be glad if you can accord me an interview when I shall be pleased to place all the facts at your disposal and therefore hold myself at your service.

Yours sincerely
J F Benton

The Rt Hon D Lloyd George, MP   **25th February 1916**

6 Whitehall Gardens, S W

Referring to my letter of 3rd July, last year to which you kindly replied on 20th July, suggesting that my brother should submit his invention to the Admiralty or the War Office. I am now writing to ask your further advice in the light of his experience after doing so. He approached the War Office whose representatives inspected his machine at the improvements of which they evinced great pleasure and inspected drawings etc, with outcome the War Office refused to consider the matter. In the meantime he had been proceeding with his researches and evolved a new wing which could be fitted to all existing machines and which will increase their speed by somewhere about a fifth and in the way which I have just read that Graham White forecasts as desirable. On the advice of a friend in the flying world he approached Messrs Vickers who were desirous of adopting this new innovation and elaborating it under his direction, but he felt that the Government should have the opportunity of taking it up themselves and therefore approached the Admiralty confidentially. After an examination of his complete drawings the Board of Inventions have notified him that they neither wish to consider purchasing or even to experiment with the design. It seems to me that if a firm of Vickers standing consider it worthwhile that surely it would be worth the Government's while and effect economy. Incidentally I may mention that with regard to the Invention which was submitted to the War Office and refused by them, a few weeks afterwards my brother was told by the editor of a paper that his design was being experimented with at Farnborough (after they had refused him) and he now hears that firms have orders to construct on his principle. As the procedure seems similar in the present case of the Admiralty as with the War Office it seems quite likely that the same thing may happen again and if so it seems to me not only to be dishonest but what is sometimes another thing contrary to public policy. I shall be glad if you can suggest any way by which the matter may be re-opened and just treatment meted out.

This present war is truly so terrible that we want brainy and clever men to help our country, my brother is so disheartened that yesterday he tried to enlist as an ordinary soldier. Think of his knowledge in the flying world, he is a born inventor and one never knows how his original ideas may not help us – I wish you could interview him personally, do try for he could do well explain and show you things.

Yours sincerely
Carrie Harker

Ministry of Munitions of War

6 Whitehall Gardens, S W

28th February 1916

Dear Madam

Mr Lloyd George desires me to thank you for your letter of the 25th instant regarding Mr John Benton, your brother. I am to express regret that his negotiations with the Admiralty and the War Office have not had a result more satisfactory to him.

I am to add that, as you will realise, the work in question in no way falls under the Ministry of Munitions. I am to state however that we are making special enquiries at the War Office with regard to the whole matter and hope to let you know the result as soon as we hear from them.

Yours faithfully
Wm Sutherland

31st March 1916   Green Lane Engineering Works
                                       Bray Road
                                       Maidenhead, Berkshire

On 25th June 1915 a letter was written to Mr Lloyd George, telling him that I had seven years practical experience in building and flying my own machines and that the present one now in my hangar was my sixth and that I was anxious to show the machine to a Government representative. Evidently Mr Lloyd George passed on my letter to the War Office for it was acknowledged by them on 23rd July, following which they wrote advising me that representatives would be sent to inspect my machine.

- A. On 5th August, Captain Hooper and lieutenant inspected the machine and expressed pleasure at the design, Captain Hooper and regretted that he had not got his camera with him, he took dimensions and was given descriptive matter and copies of patents. He requested me to send on my drawings immediately to him c/o The Officer's Mess, Farnborough which I did within three days.

- B. On 17th August, a letter was received from W O Dept, MA 3 refusing to avail themselves of the machine and giving no reasons. Subsequently we went to the War Office to endeavour to clear away what we felt must be a misapprehension and consequently the matter was re-opened. Thereupon they offered the loan of an 100 hp engine for trials and requested me to make a formal application for same and at the same time send a set of drawings as they had none.

- C. On 26th August, (the next day) I wrote to Captain Hooper asking him to return the drawings which I had sent him to save time, and he replied that they had been passed on to the War Office and were only two hours in his possession.

- D. In accordance with their request (see paragraph B) I wrote to Dept M A 3 at the War Office on September 1st accepting their offer of loan of a 100 hp engine and stating that Captain Hooper sent on drawings to the War Office and if they cannot trace them I will make a further set. In reply to this letter, on 13th September I received a communication from them saying the Department did not wish to proceed further in the matter! By the same post a letter was received from Major General Hickman referring to descriptive matter and drawings received by his department (Inventions) and as I had sent no others these were the ones originally in the hands of Captain Hooper and evidently had gone astray for a time, and saying that the Department will be pleased to view the machine when it is in flying condition. I replied to Major General Hickman that as soon as I could put in a 100 hp engine I would hold myself at the convenience of his department, whereupon he replied saying the correspondence had been filed for future reference.

E. On 8th October, a well informed friend in the flying world wrote and told me positively that the RAF authorities were experimenting on their own account with a machine built upon my designs but with at that time indifferent success – difficulties (due to insufficiency of data) were evidently ultimately overcome, for in January I learnt from an old employee now engaged in an aeroplane works that his firm among others are at the moment engaged in making a large number of wings of my design to go on existing machines, and about the same time information reached me that the chassis of my machine had been adopted for seaplanes and was being manufactured for the Government. The further necessary data which overcame the difficulties of the RAF were supplied by me at a subsequent interview with Professor Hopkinson at Victory House (further mention of which is made below) when I gave him the necessary particulars which he forwarded to Mr O'Gorman with my knowledge and consent.

F. In the first days of October I had the privilege of meeting a well known engineering expert who inspected my machine and forthwith gave me an introduction to Professor Hopkinson of the Admiralty Board of Invention saying that he considered my inventions merited their attention. Particulars were sent to Professor Hopkinson at his request and ultimately an interview was arranged for 8th November. In the meantime I had completed a further departure in aeroplane construction (variable wings) in effect the major desideratum of flying men, and at this interview I described in detail to him my existing machine and also told him of my latest invention (without going into details). Professor Hopkinson said that he would see that my proposals were considered by the Admiralty Board of Invention and also if I would let him have the necessary written descriptions and drawings he would place same with Mr O'Gorman at Farnborough personally, which was done and is referred to in paragraph E.

G. Subsequent to this interview I wrote to the friend mentioned in paragraph E telling him what was, and had been done, and on 24th November I received a reply from him, from which I gave a verbatim extract: "I am rather sorry to hear that your new designs are going to the RAF because that simply you are liable to the same treatment that other people have to suffer, which judging from previous experiences seems to be that an idea is studied carefully by the people there, anything original is noted for further use and the inventor is simply told his idea is impracticable or at any rate that it cannot be used, then some months afterwards the factory itself comes out with the same idea more or less and takes the credit for itself".

H. In due course the Admiralty Board of Invention met and examined my drawings etc, and in the outcome Professor Hopkinson wrote to me to say that the Board had rejected my proposals, that they asked him if he saw any reason why they should reconsider their decision and that he replied "no" giving certain reasons evidently originated with Mr O'Gorman (for as you have seen despite the honest decision of Professor Hopkinson and his Board, two parts at least of the invention have been adopted through the RAF), Professor Hopkinson added that he had advised them however to go further into the matter of my new variable area wing invention "which may have considerable importance".

I. Before submitting the full particulars and working drawings I then endeavoured to obtain a certificate enabling me to take out a secret patent as in the light of my previous experiences and the importance of the invention I naturally wanted every possible safeguard for secrecy. After considerable correspondence I was informed by the Board that they could not grant a certificate without first having the full description but if I would send that to them it would be in strict confidence. In view of this I wrote asking for an appointment when I would personally place my drawings etc before their representative and eventually on14th February I was enabled to do so.

J. Following this interview at which I fully explained the details, the aeroplane and seaplane subcommittees met for its consideration and afterwards I was informed "that neither subcommittee would recommend the proposal for adoption or experiment". In view of the fact that the Board were advised that the invention may have considerable importance (see paragraph H) it seems curious that even if not straight away adopted they should bar themselves from experiment.

K. I wrote asking for reasons for the decision and a reply dated 24th February stating that "a system for altering the area of the wings of an aeroplane is not of sufficient value at the present time (!) to justify the complicated mechanism and additional weight which would be entailed by its adoption". This again although a generalisation is contrary to the expert advice given them. They go on to make certain statements which refer to my design which being of a technical nature and wholly theoretical can only be proved or disproved by actual experiment which their action has barred.

John F Benton
31st March 1916

For the use of Sir Gilbert Parker, MP　　　　Green Lane Engineering Works
"Bankside", Bray Road
Maidenhead, Berkshire
6th May 1916

The nature of the invention acquired by the Government is:–
A wing, the ends of which can be washed out in camber and angle of attack while flying, the method and design of which is covered by Patent No 10487/15.

The invention was disclosed to the War Office representatives from Farnborough on 5th August 1915, whereupon the RAF within our knowledge but without our consent, carried out experiments with no success owing to insufficiency of data. These data reached them later through Professor Hopkinson and the editor of "Aeroplane" when they must have been successful for following this, orders for 600 were placed with the Whitehead Aircraft Company, Richmond and other firms. We received this information on 11th February 1916 through an old employee who is now engaged at the above works. He further told us that his firm were making these wings to fit to existing machines to be used at the Front.

When Captain Hooper and a lieutenant (the War Office representatives) came to Chalvey (5th August 1915) they were struck by the novelty of the device.

per pro Green Lane Engineeing Works
John F Benton

Miss Margaret McMillan　　　　Green Lane Engineering Works
"Bankside", Bray Road
Maidenhead, Berkshire
30th May 1916

Dear Miss McMillan

Thank you very much for your letters to Mr Henderson. No we have not heard anything from him; I feel disappointed particularly since I was looking forward to his report which you remember they said was practically ready to be sent to us the next day. In any case I should like Mr Henderson to return the correspondence and I will write him if you advise this but I think it would be better done by you, if I may trouble you. Next I owe you an apology and explanation for not writing immediately, we came straight from the War Office, after seeing General Mc Innis' representative, to the clinic at an inopportune time and since then I have started making munitions here and I barely get time to write a letter. We are now turning out about 25,000 rifle grenade pieces a week, I shall be very pleased to show you the girls at work when you come down again. For the time being I have to be right on the spot teaching them. A few days after the visit of Lt Thurston to the hangar of which I wrote you in the last letter, we were asked to come up to General Mc Innes' department, Albemarle Street to discuss their proposals. I met Captain Clarke and Colonel Beautty there and the arrangement we came to is that the War Office is to immediately make up a set of the wings (as at Chalvey) and try them on their own machines at the Central Flying School, Uphaven (near Devizes) and we are to see the results there.

They discourage the use of these wings for variable speed but said they want them as an air brake. I very much wanted a machine with engine at Chalvey to fit my latest wings to but they want to make this conditional on the success of their Uphaven experiments. They say financial help could only be given to us as an advance on a contract which they would do if they place a contract with us. If you are coming to Maidenhead at Whitsun please call and have tea with us, Peter and Tot will be able to play to their hearts content.

With my kindest regards
Yours sincerely
J F Benton

Mr A Henderson,
President of the Board of Education,
Whitehall, S W

Benton Munitions

8th August 1916

Dear Miss McMillan

Many thanks for your letter enclosing summary, and please accept my renewed thanks for your untiring efforts on my behalf. I wish that the War Office aeroplane department had been so zealous for their country in this matter as you, but I am afraid we are either forgotten or being treated lightly. I can no longer see what useful purpose it can serve for Mr Henderson to retain our correspondence since nothing is being done and so far as we are aware the position remains unchanged. We have heard nothing further from General McInnes, please remember me to your sister and tell Peter and Tot I am coming to see them next week. I should very much like to come on Wednesday the 16th, inst, will you be at home in the afternoon? I am very busy at my new works, so much so that I often cannot afford the time to cycle to Mrs Allen's house for meals. My sister and Iris have left for their holidays and they wished to be remembered to you both. It will give me a great deal of pleasure to shew you my works when you come to Maidenhead and yet every machine which flies overhead makes me long for my aeroplane works. You will understand Miss McMillan there is very little soul in making munition parts, but every flying machine has an individuality to the builder. If I had the capital I should approach the War Office offering to build machines after their own pattern and then perhaps I could eventually bring in and obtain remuneration for my own designs and past patents. If you will excuse my seeming egotism I feel more confident than ever, that aeroplane works under my control would be of great use to the nation because so far I have had the long experience of the experimental side and now organisation, for in a few short weeks and with practically no money at all I have some 50 employees at work and another 50 in premises adjoining which I have installed for another firm under Mrs Allen. I am turning out munitions that run into over a hundred thousand per week including timers to rifle grenades, 18 pounders and so on. We have already delivered several millions. This time must make a point not to forget to bring Peter's model with me or he will not attach much reality to my promises in future! I am writing this at home and it is getting very early in the morning so I had better stop.

With very kind regards
Yours sincerely
J F Benton

Mr A Henderson
President of the Board of Education
Whitehall, S W

Inventions Board

Lord Fisher's colleagues and helpers

Arrangements for the organisation of the Inventions Board, of which Lord Fisher was appointed chairman on July 5th, have now been completed. The Board is to assist the Admiralty in co-ordinating and encouraging scientific effort in relation to the requirements of the Naval Service.

The Board will comprise a Central Committee and a panel of consultants, composed of scientific experts, who will advise the main Committee on questions referred to them.

Central Committee

Lord Fisher (President)
Sir J J Thomson, O M, F R S, Physicist
Sir C A Parsons, KC B, F R S, Turbine expert
Mr G T Beilby, F R S, Fuel expert

Consulting Panel

Professor H B Baker, F R S, Chemist
Professor W H Bragg, F R S, Physicist
Professor H C H Carpenter, Metallurgist
Sir William Crookes, O M, F R S, Chemist and Physicist
Mr W Dudell, F R S, Engineer
Professor Percy Frankland, F R S, Chemist
Professor Bertram Hopkinson, F R S, Engineer
Sir Oliver Lodge, F R S, Physicist
Professor W J Pope, F R S, Chemist
Sir Ernest Rutherford, F R S, Radium expert
Mr G Gerald Stoney, F R S, Enginer
Professor R J Strutt, F R S, Physicist

This Board may be added to.

The Board is accommodated temporarily in the Whitehall Rooms, Hotel Metropole, Whitehall Place, S W, but at an early date will be transferred to permanent offices at Victory House, Cockspur Street, S W.

Communications should be addressed to the Secretary, Board of Invention and Research.

Conclusion

After his sister and her daughter had gone to America, Johnny had another fling in the invention business, in, of all things, articles of adornment for women. The idea was cleverly based on what today would be "plastics", Johnny used fish bones, he realised that these were virtually waste material, were extremely durable, could be cut into shapes, glued together and painted. An explanatory diagram and a copy of the patent is in the appendix. The idea was a success, the product was sold through Liberty"s, the West End store and repeat orders were gained, however, the scheme "petered" out because Johnny could not take the repetitive work and another idea bit the dust!

It was during this period, the early 20's, that he and Rose Allen embarked upon the "Good" Life, they went in for rearing goats, kept chickens and bees and of course raised vegetables, becoming more or less self–sufficient for food.

Around 1928, the Sunlight Soap people launched a "soap with coupons" campaign, you bought your soap, collected the coupons and put in for the prizes. The top prize was a magnificent Clyno car, which no doubt Sunlight thought to be quite unattainable. Not so Johnny! He bought a very large quantity of the soap, devised a means of converting it into soap flakes, sold the flakes back to the wholesaler, sent in the coupons and drove off with the car!

His great friend Wally Roberts, who, with the help of his wife Florrie had built up their egg producing business, expanded out to a place at Tilehurst near Reading. In the mid–thirties Johnny was always at the farm and made a very substantial contribution by devising a method of packaging the eggs and since by this time the Roberts were sending their eggs all over the country, Johnny introduced a significant improvement to the operation. It was in the late 30's and just before World War II that Johnny began his faith healing circle in the Reading area – again with his friends the Roberts to help him – the "technique" involved the laying on of hands. Johnny had two gloves, one red and one blue, one for each hand and he would place his red gloved hand on the painful spot and then make to sweep away the pain with the blue glove, all the while the circle would pray loudly for the healing of the affliction.

There was an element of hypnosis in these proceedings, Johnny had been dabbling in this practice for some years – he had a go at everything going on at the time and hypnosis was all the rage in the theatre then until it was stopped.

When war came he and his dear friend Mrs Allen slipped into retirement relying more and more on the help of others thus they passed into the protection and security of their home and garden at Lane End.

Grandma Allen, as she was so affectionately known, used to make shaped bowls and pots from old 78 gramophone records, she found that when these were carefully warmed in an oven they could be easily moulded to any suitable shape – she was a clever little soul, Johnny used to call her "Little Mummy", they were always happy, working hard together and motoring along the country lanes in their little black Clyno car.

They went out on picnics and visited all their friends, such happy days to end their lives so well fulfilled.

Appendix 3

1. The Patent taken out by J Benton referring to "Articles of adornment and method of producing same".

Patents and Design Acts, 1907 and 1919   **1st March 1921**

Provisional Application

"Articles of adornment and method of producing same".

I, JOHN FREDERICK BENTON, Engineer, of Ford House, Pinkey's Green, Maidenhead in the County of Berks, a British subject, do hereby declare the nature of this invention to be as follows:–

This invention relates to novel articles of adornment and method of producing same and comprises the production of an infinite variety of such articles of highly artistic appearance, particularly for the ornament of ladies millinery or dress or for use as jewellery or similar purposes. In carrying out the invention I utilise the bones of a large variety of fish of any kinds which may be readily available and after having cleansed same as by immersion or washing in hot water they are taken either in their natural shape or pieced together built up or fashioned as by cutting or shaping to produce the design required such as a bird, butterfly, wing or plume, or aeroplane to the fancy of the designer.

Having produced the design required in the rough it is then painted, preferably using oil colours for the purpose, with which there is suitably mixed a medium such as mcgylp in relatively large proportion, the colouring applied being appropriate to the design under treatment and being determined by the artistic skill of the producer. A transparent varnish may be finally applied if considered desirable.

The results obtained by the method and with the use of the materials mentioned are of extremely pleasing effect, resembling in finish high class enamel or cloisonne work with a translucent and irridescent appearance, the articles produced being also very light in weight without being unduly fragile. Finally the articles may be further ornamented where appropriate, by the application thereto at suitable places of real or artificial jewels, stones, or the like.

Provisional Patent Application No 2820, dated January 21st 1921.
Officially accepted by the Patent Office on February 25th 1921